A Shorter Alternative Service Book

Services from The Alternative Service Book 1980

*Authorized for use in the Church of England
in conjunction with The Book of Common Prayer*

Cambridge University Press

Hodder & Stoughton

Oxford University Press

SPCK

Printed in England by Clays Ltd, St Ives plc

Jointly published by:

Cambridge University Press, The Edinburgh Building, Shaftesbury Road, Cambridge CB2 2RU

Hodder & Stoughton Ltd, Mill Road, Dunton Green, Sevenoaks, Kent TN13 2YA

Oxford University Press, Walton Street, Oxford OX2 6DP

SPCK: The Society for Promoting Christian Knowledge, Holy Trinity Church, Marylebone Road, London NW1 4DU

ISBNs

CUP: 0 521 50769 3

Hodder & Stoughton: 0 340 54942 4

OUP: 0 19 146165 2

SPCK: 0 281 04505 4

British Library cataloguing in publication data

Church of England. *Liturgy and ritual*
A Shorter Alternative Service Book
I. Title
264'.03   BX5147.03

CONTENTS

Authorization [7]

Preface [9]

General Notes 31–32

Morning and Evening Prayer 45–70
Morning Prayer 48
Evening Prayer 61

Prayers for Various Occasions 97–107

The Order for Holy Communion Rite A 113–173
The Order following the pattern of the
  Book of Common Prayer 146
Appendices 154

The Order for Holy Communion Rite B 175–210
Appendices 201

Initiation Services 211–222 241–249
Thanksgiving for the Birth of a Child 213
Thanksgiving after Adoption 218

The Baptism of Children 241

Copyright [251]

*Please note that the page numbering does not run continuously but follows that of **The Alternative Service Book 1980**.*

*Cross references to pages not included in this book refer to **The Alternative Service Book 1980**.*

A Shorter Alternative Service Book

AUTHORIZATION

The Services of *The Alternative Service Book 1980*, together with the Calendar, Rules to Order the Service, and Lectionary, are authorized pursuant to Canon B2 of the Canons of the Church of England for use from the date of publication of The Alternative Service Book until 31 December 2000.

Decisions as to which of the authorized services are to be used (other than occasional offices) shall be taken jointly by the incumbent and the parochial church council; in the case of occasional offices (other than Confirmation and Ordination), the decision is to be made by the minister conducting the service, subject to the right of any of the persons concerned to object beforehand to its use; in the case of Confirmation and Ordination services, the decision lies with the confirming or presiding bishop.

The versions of the Psalter which are authorized for use in conjunction with the services of *The Alternative Service Book 1980* are the Prayer Book Psalter, The Revised Psalter, the Liturgical Psalter, and the Grail Psalter.

Preface by
The Archbishop of Canterbury

The Alternative Service Book 1980 has proved its worth since publication in the vast majority of parishes in England.

In many cases there has been a demand for the most commonly used services to be available in a properly bound book, and *A Shorter Alternative Service Book* will be widely welcomed on this account. The page numbering follows that of the complete *ASB*, and therefore, *A Shorter ASB* will be usable alongside copies of the larger book.

I very much welcome this publication and commend it to the Church wholeheartedly.

 GEORGE CANTUAR

General Notes

1 **Distinctions in the Text** Sections of services with numbers in blue may be omitted. Where a number of options are included in a mandatory part of a service, the rubric governing the options is numbered in black, but the texts themselves are numbered in blue. Texts in bold type are to be said by the congregation.

2 **Saying and Singing** Where rubrics indicate that a section is to be 'said', this must be understood to include 'or sung' and vice versa.

3 **Posture** Wherever a certain posture is particularly appropriate, it is indicated in the left-hand margin. At all other points local custom may be established and followed.

4 **Biblical Passages** The sentences, psalms, and readings may be read in any duly authorized version.

5 **Prayer Book Texts** Where parts of a service are sung to well-known settings, the traditional words for which they were composed may be used.

6 **The Lord's Prayer** On any occasion the Lord's Prayer may be used in its modern form (as in Holy Communion Rite A p. 142), or in its modified form (as in Holy Communion Rite B p. 196), or in its traditional form (as in the Book of Common Prayer).

7 **Collects** On any occasion when more than one collect is provided (pp. 398 ff.), only one need be used.

8 **Collect Endings** In the case of any collect ending with the words 'Christ our Lord', the Minister may at his discretion add the longer ending:
'who is alive and reigns with you and the Holy Spirit, one God, now and for ever.'

9 **Hymns** Various points are indicated for the singing of hymns; but, if occasion requires, they may be sung at other points also.

Morning Prayer
and
Evening Prayer

NOTES

1   **Interchangeability** Either form of Morning Prayer and of Evening Prayer may be used on Sundays or weekdays; but the full form is recommended for use on Sundays.

2   **Sentences** Sentences for use on Sundays, other Holy Days and special occasions are included with the collects and readings (pp. 398 ff.). There is a further selection on pages 37-42.

3   **Penitence** Sections 3-7 (pp. 48, 49), 26-30 (pp. 61, 62), 63-67 (pp. 82, 83), may be used at a later point in the service after the collects.

4   **The Absolution** In the absence of a priest, 'us' and 'our' are said instead of 'you' and 'your' at sections 6, 29, and 66.

5   **Venite** The whole of Psalm 95 may be said instead of the form at sections 9 and 53.

6   **The Psalms** The psalms to be read each day are as appointed in Table 1 (pp. 983 ff.), or Table 2 (pp. 1047, 1048).

7   **The Readings** The readings should be announced in the order: book, chapter, verse.

8   **Readings at Holy Communion** If Holy Communion is to follow immediately, two or three readings may be used. When three readings are used, the New Testament reading will be read at sections 13 or 36, and the Gospel after sections 15 or 38. The Sermon will follow the Gospel.

9   **Canticles in Advent and Lent** Saviour of the World and the last five verses of Te Deum are particularly suitable for use in Advent and Lent.

10 **The Litany** The Litany (pp. 99-102) may be said instead of sections 17-23 or 40-46 followed by the Lord's Prayer, the Collect of the Day, and the Grace.

Sentences

GENERAL

Seek the Lord while he may be found; call upon him while he is near. *Isaiah 55.6*

God is spirit, and those who worship him must worship in spirit and in truth. *John 4.24*

In everything make your requests known to God in prayer and petition with thanksgiving. *Philippians 4.6*

Through Jesus let us continually offer up to God the sacrifice of praise, that is, the tribute of lips which acknowledge his name. *Hebrews 13.15*

To God, the only God, who saves us through Jesus Christ our Lord, be glory and majesty, dominion and authority, before all time and now and for ever. *Jude 25*

TIMES OF THANKSGIVING

Give thanks to the Lord, and call upon his name; tell the nations all that he has done. *Psalm 105.1*

Let the nations be glad and sing; for God judges the people with righteousness and governs the nations upon earth. *Psalm 67.4*

TIMES OF TROUBLE

God is our refuge and strength, an ever present help in trouble. *Psalm 46.1*

Morning Prayer

1 **Stand**
The minister may say

> We have come together as the family of God
>   in our Father's presence
> to offer him praise and thanksgiving,
> to hear and receive his holy word,
> to bring before him the needs of the world,
> to ask his forgiveness of our sins,
> and to seek his grace,
> that through his Son Jesus Christ
> we may give ourselves to his service.

2 A SENTENCE OF SCRIPTURE may be said (see p. 46) and
A HYMN may be sung.

3 The minister may say

> If we say we have no sin, we deceive ourselves,
> and the truth is not in us. If we confess our sins,
> God is faithful and just, and will forgive us our
> sins, and cleanse us from all unrighteousness.

or the sentences for Ash Wednesday to Lent 5 may be used.

4 The minister may say

> Let us confess our sins to almighty God.

5 **Kneel**
All　　**Almighty God, our heavenly Father,**
we have sinned against you and against our
**　　fellow men,**
in thought and word and deed,
through negligence, through weakness,
through our own deliberate fault.

We are truly sorry
and repent of all our sins.
For the sake of your Son Jesus Christ, who
    died for us,
forgive us all that is past;
and grant that we may serve you in newness
    of life
to the glory of your name. Amen.

6 Priest   Almighty God,
           who forgives all who truly repent,
           have mercy upon *you*,
           pardon and deliver *you* from all *your* sins,
           confirm and strengthen *you* in all goodness,
           and keep *you* in life eternal;
           through Jesus Christ our Lord. **Amen.**

7 Instead of section 5 one of the alternative Confessions may
   be used (pp. 165, 166).

8 **Stand**
   Minister   O Lord, open our lips;
   People   **and our mouth shall proclaim your praise.**

   Minister   Let us worship the Lord.
   People   **All praise to his name.**

   All   **Glory to the Father, and to the Son,**
              and to the Holy Spirit:
              as it was in the beginning, is now,
              and shall be for ever. Amen.

9 VENITE, or JUBILATE, or THE EASTER ANTHEMS (which
   shall always be used on Easter Day)

   VENITE
1 **O come let us sing** ᐧ **out · to the** ᐧ **Lord:**
     let us shout in triumph to the ᐧ **rock of** ᐧ **our sal** ᐧ **vation.**

2   Let us come before his | face with | thanksgiving:
     and cry | out to · him | joyfully · in | psalms.

3   For the Lord is a | great | God:
     and a great | king a·bove | all | gods.

4   In his hand are the | depths · of the | earth:
     and the peaks of the | mountains · are | his | also.

†5   The sea is his and | he | made it:
     his hands | moulded | dry | land.

6   Come let us worship and | bow | down:
     and kneel be|fore the | Lord our | maker.

7   For he is the | Lord our | God:
     we are his | people · and the | sheep of · his |
     pasture.

8   If only you would hear his | voice to|day:
     for he | comes to | judge the | earth.

9   He shall judge the | world with | righteousness:
     and the | peoples | with his | truth.

    Glory to the Father and | to the | Son:
     and | to the | Holy | Spirit;
    as it was in the be|ginning is | now:
     and shall be for | ever. | A|men.

JUBILATE

1   O shout to the Lord in triumph | all the | earth:
     serve the Lord with gladness
     and come before his | face with | songs of | joy.

2   Know that the Lord | he is | God:
     it is he who has made us and we are his
     we are his | people · and the | sheep of · his |
     pasture.

3   Come into his gates with thanksgiving
     and into his | courts with | praise:
     give thanks to him and | bless his | holy | name.

4   For the Lord is good * his loving mercy | is for | ever:
     his faithfulness through|out all | gener|ations.

Glory to the Father and ˈ to the ˈ Son:
    and ˈ to the ˈ Holy ˈ Spirit;
as it was in the beˈginning is ˈ now:
    and shall be for ˈever. ˈAˈmen.

THE EASTER ANTHEMS

1 Christ our passover has been ˈ sacri·ficed ˈ for us:
    so let us ˈ celeˈbrate the ˈ feast,

2 not with the old leaven of corˈruption · and ˈ wickedness:
    but with the unleavened ˈ bread of · sinˈcerity · and ˈ truth.

3 Christ once raised from the dead ˈ dies no ˈ more:
    death has no ˈ more doˈminion ˈ over him.

4 In dying he died to sin ˈ once for ˈ all:
    in ˈ living · he ˈ lives to ˈ God.

5 See yourselves therefore as ˈ dead to ˈ sin:
    and alive to God in ˈ Jesus ˈ Christ our ˈ Lord.

6 Christ has been ˈ raised · from the ˈ dead:
    the ˈ firstfruits · of ˈ those who ˈ sleep.

7 For as by ˈ man came ˈ death:
    by man has come also the resurˈrection ˈ of the ˈ dead;

8 for as in ˈ Adam · all ˈ die:
    even so in Christ shall ˈ all be ˈ made aˈlive.

Glory to the Father and ˈ to the ˈ Son:
    and ˈ to the ˈ Holy ˈ Spirit;
as it was in the beˈginning is ˈ now:
    and shall be for ˈever. ˈAˈmen.

10 THE PSALMS appointed
Each psalm or group of psalms ends with

Glory to the Father and ˈ to the ˈ Son:
    and ˈ to the ˈ Holy ˈ Spirit;
as it was in the beˈginning is ˈ now:
    and shall be for ˈever. ˈAˈmen.

11 **Sit**

THE FIRST READING, from the Old Testament

At the end the reader may say

       This is the word of the Lord.
All   **Thanks be to God.**

Silence may be kept.

12 **Stand**
BENEDICTUS, or A SONG OF CREATION,
or GREAT AND WONDERFUL

BENEDICTUS (The Song of Zechariah)

1 **Blessèd be the Lord the ˈ God of ˈ Israel:**
   for he has come to his ˈ people · and ˈ set them ˈ free.

2 **He has raised up for us a ˈ mighty ˈ saviour:**
   born of the ˈ house · of his ˈ servant ˈ David.

3 **Through his holy prophets he ˈ promised · of ˈ old:**
   that he would save us from our enemies
   from the ˈ hands of ˈ all that ˈ hate us.

4 **He promised to show ˈ mercy · to our ˈ fathers:**
   and to re ˈ member · his ˈ holy ˈ covenant.

5 **This was the oath he swore to our ˈ father ˈ Abraham:**
   to set us ˈ free · from the ˈ hands of · our ˈ enemies,

6 **free to worship him with ˈ out ˈ fear:**
   holy and righteous in his sight ˈ all the ˈ days of ·
   our ˈ life.

7 **You my child shall be called the prophet of the ˈ**
Most ˈ High:
   for you will go before the ˈ Lord · to pre ˈ pare his ˈ way,

8 **to give his people knowledge ˈ of sal ˈ vation:**
   by the for ˈ giveness · of ˈ all their ˈ sins.

9 **In the tender compassion ˈ of our ˈ God:**
   the dawn from on ˈ high shall ˈ break up ˈ on us,

10   to shine on those who dwell in darkness and the |
shadow · of | death:
    and to guide our feet | into · the | way of | peace.

Glory to the Father and | to the | Son:
    and | to the | Holy | Spirit;
as it was in the be|ginning is | now:
    and shall be for | ever. | A|men.

A SONG OF CREATION

On weekdays vv. 4-17 may be omitted.

1   Bless the Lord all cre|ated | things:
    sing his | praise · and ex|alt him · for | ever.

2   Bless the | Lord you | heavens:
    sing his | praise · and ex|alt him · for | ever.

3   Bless the Lord you | angels · of the | Lord:
    bless the | Lord all | you his | hosts;

4   bless the Lord you waters a|bove the | heavens:
    sing his | praise · and ex|alt him · for | ever.

5   Bless the Lord | sun and | moon:
    bless the | Lord you | stars of | heaven;

6   bless the Lord all | rain and | dew:
    sing his | praise · and ex|alt him · for | ever.

7   Bless the Lord all | winds that | blow:
    bless the | Lord you | fire and | heat;

8   bless the Lord scorching wind and | bitter | cold:
    sing his | praise · and ex|alt him · for | ever.

9   Bless the Lord dews and | falling | snows:
    bless the | Lord you | nights and | days;

10   bless the Lord | light and | darkness:
    sing his | praise · and ex|alt him · for | ever.

11   Bless the Lord | frost and | cold:
    bless the | Lord you | ice and | snow;

12   bless the Lord | lightnings · and | clouds:
    sing his | praise · and ex|alt him · for | ever.

13   O let the earth | bless the | Lord:
      bless the | Lord you | mountains · and | hills;

14   bless the Lord all that | grows · in the | ground:
      sing his | praise · and ex|alt him · for | ever.

15   Bless the | Lord you | springs:
      bless the | Lord you | seas and | rivers;

16   bless the Lord you whales and all that | swim · in the | waters:
      sing his | praise · and ex|alt him · for | ever.

17   Bless the Lord all | birds · of the | air:
      bless the | Lord you | beasts and | cattle;

18   bless the Lord all | men · on the | earth:
      sing his | praise · and ex|alt him · for | ever.

19   O People of God | bless the | Lord:
      bless the | Lord you | priests · of the | Lord;

20   bless the Lord you | servants · of the | Lord:
      sing his | praise · and ex|alt him · for | ever.

21   Bless the Lord all men of | upright | spirit:
      bless the Lord you that are | holy · and | humble · in | heart.

      Bless the Father the Son and the | Holy | Spirit:
      sing his | praise · and ex|alt him · for | ever.

GREAT AND WONDERFUL

1   Great and wonderful are your deeds Lord | God · the Al|mighty:
      just and true are your | ways O | King · of the | nations.

2   Who shall not revere and praise your | name O | Lord?
      for | you a|lone are | holy.

3   All nations shall come and worship | in your | presence:
      for your just | dealings · have | been re|vealed.

      To him who sits on the throne | and · to the | Lamb:
      be praise and honour glory and might
      for ever and | ever. | A|men.

13 **Sit**
THE SECOND READING, from the New Testament

At the end the reader may say

> This is the word of the Lord.

All **Thanks be to God.**

Silence may be kept.

14 · A SERMON may be preached here, or at the end of the
service.

15 **Stand**
TE DEUM, or GLORIA IN EXCELSIS or, in Lent, SAVIOUR
OF THE WORLD

TE DEUM
Verses 14-18 may be omitted.

1 **You are ⏐ God · and we ⏐ praise you:**
   you are the ⏐ Lord and ⏐ we ac⏐claim you;

2 **you are the e⏐ternal ⏐ Father:**
   all cre⏐ation ⏐ worships ⏐ you.

3 **To you all angels * all the ⏐ powers of ⏐ heaven:**
   cherubim and seraphim ⏐ sing in ⏐ endless ⏐ praise,

4 **Holy holy holy Lord * God of ⏐ power and ⏐ might:**
   heaven and ⏐ earth are ⏐ full of · your ⏐ glory.

5 **The glorious company of ap⏐ostles ⏐ praise you:**
   the noble fellowship of prophets praise you
   the white-robed ⏐ army · of ⏐ martyrs ⏐ praise you.

6 **Throughout the world the holy ⏐ Church ac⏐claims you:**
   Father of ⏐ majes⏐ty un⏐bounded;

(†) 7 **your true and only Son * worthy of ⏐ all ⏐ worship:**
   and the Holy ⏐ Spirit ⏐ advocate · and ⏐ guide.

8 **You Christ are the ⏐ King of ⏐ glory:**
   the e⏐ternal ⏐ Son · of the ⏐ Father.

9   When you became man to ˈ set us ˈ free:
      you did not abˈhor the ˈ Virgin's ˈ womb.

10 You overcame the ˈ sting of ˈ death:
      and opened the kingdom of ˈ heaven · to ˈ all beˈlievers.

11 You are seated at God's right ˈ hand in ˈ glory:
      we believe that you will ˈ come and ˈ be our ˈ judge.

12 Come then Lord and ˈ help your ˈ people:
      bought with the ˈ price of ˈ your own ˈ blood;

13 and bring us ˈ with your ˈ saints:
      to ˈ glory ˈ everˈlasting.

14 Save your people Lord and ˈ bless · your inˈheritance:
      govern and upˈhold them ˈ now and ˈ always.

15 Day by ˈ day we ˈ bless you:
      we ˈ praise your ˈ name for ˈ ever.

16 Keep us today Lord from ˈ all ˈ sin:
      have mercy ˈ on us ˈ Lord have ˈ mercy.

17 Lord show us your ˈ love and ˈ mercy:
      for we ˈ put our ˈ trust in ˈ you.

(†) 18 In you Lord ˈ is our ˈ hope:
      let us not be conˈfounded ˈ at the ˈ last.

GLORIA IN EXCELSIS
1   Glory to ˈ God · in the ˈ highest:
      and ˈ peace · to his ˈ people · on ˈ earth.

2   Lord God ˈ heaven·ly ˈ King:
      alˈmighty ˈ God and ˈ Father,

3   we worship you we ˈ give you ˈ thanks:
      we ˈ praise you ˈ for your ˈ glory.

4   Lord Jesus Christ only ˈ Son · of the ˈ Father:
      Lord ˈ God ˈ Lamb of ˈ God,

5   you take away the ˈ sin · of the ˈ world:
      have ˈ mercy ˈ on ˈ us;

6   you are seated at the right hand ǀ of the ǀ Father:
     re ǀceive ǀ our ǀ prayer.

7   For you a ǀlone · are the ǀ Holy One:
     you a ǀlone ǀ are the ǀ Lord,

8   you alone are the Most High
     Jesus Christ with the ǀ Holy ǀ Spirit:
     in the glory of God the ǀ Father. ǀ A ǀmen.

SAVIOUR OF THE WORLD

1   Jesus saviour of the world * come to us ǀ in your ǀ mercy:
     we look to ǀ you to ǀ save and ǀ help us.

2   By your cross and your life laid down
     you set your ǀ people ǀ free:
     we look to ǀ you to ǀ save and ǀ help us.

3   When they were ready to perish you ǀ
     saved · your dis ǀciples:
     we look to ǀ you to ǀ come to · our ǀ help.

4   In the greatness of your mercy loose us ǀ from our ǀ
     chains:
     forgive the ǀ sins of ǀ all your ǀ people.

5   Make yourself known as our saviour and ǀ
     mighty · de ǀliverer:
     save and ǀ help us · that ǀ we may ǀ praise you.

6   Come now and dwell with us ǀ Lord Christ ǀ Jesus:
     hear our ǀ prayer · and be ǀ with us ǀ always.

(†) 7 And when you ǀ come in · your ǀ glory:
     make us to be one with you * and to ǀ share the ǀ
     life of · your ǀ kingdom.

16   THE APOSTLES' CREED

     All   I believe in God, the Father almighty,
                 creator of heaven and earth.

                 I believe in Jesus Christ, his only Son,
                 our Lord.

He was conceived by the power of the
    Holy Spirit
and born of the Virgin Mary.
He suffered under Pontius Pilate,
was crucified, died, and was buried.
He descended to the dead.
On the third day he rose again.
He ascended into heaven,
and is seated at the right hand
    of the Father.
He will come again to judge the living
    and the dead.

I believe in the Holy Spirit,
the holy catholic Church,
the communion of saints,
the forgiveness of sins,
the resurrection of the body,
and the life everlasting. Amen.

17 **Kneel**
The minister may say

	Lord, have mercy upon us.
People	**Christ, have mercy upon us.**
Minister	Lord, have mercy upon us.

18 **All**

Our Father in heaven,
hallowed be your name,
your kingdom come,
your will be done,
on earth as in heaven.
Give us today our daily bread.
Forgive us our sins
as we forgive those
    who sin against us.
Lead us not into temptation
but deliver us from evil.

For the kingdom, the power,
    and the glory are yours
now and for ever. Amen.

or

Our Father, who art in heaven,
hallowed be thy name;
thy kingdom come;
thy will be done;
on earth as it is in heaven.
Give us this day our daily bread.
And forgive us our trespasses,
as we forgive those
    who trespass against us.
And lead us not into temptation;
but deliver us from evil.

For thine is the kingdom,
    the power, and the glory,
for ever and ever. Amen.

19   These versicles and responses may be said.

Minister   Show us your mercy, O Lord;
People   **and grant us your salvation.**

Minister   O Lord, save the Queen;
People   **and teach her counsellors wisdom.**

Minister   Let your priests be clothed with righteousness;
People   **and let your servants shout for joy.**

Minister   O Lord, make your ways known upon the earth;
People   **let all nations acknowledge your saving power.**

Minister   Give your people the blessing of peace;
People   **and let your glory be over all the world.**

Minister   Make our hearts clean, O God;
People   **and renew a right spirit within us.**

20   THE COLLECT OF THE DAY

21   THIS COLLECT may be said.

> O God, the author of peace
> and lover of concord,
> to know you is eternal life,
> to serve you is perfect freedom.
> Defend us your servants
> from all assaults of our enemies;
> that we may trust in your defence,
> and not fear the power of any adversaries;
> through Jesus Christ our Lord. **Amen.**

22 ONE OF THESE COLLECTS is said.

> Almighty and everlasting Father,
> we thank you that you have brought us safely
> to the beginning of this day.
> Keep us from falling into sin
> or running into danger;
> order us in all our doings;
> and guide us to do always
> what is right in your eyes;
> through Jesus Christ our Lord. **Amen.**

or
> Eternal God and Father,
> you create us by your power
> and redeem us by your love:
> guide and strengthen us by your Spirit,
> that we may give ourselves in love and service
> to one another and to you;
> through Jesus Christ our Lord. **Amen.**

23 Here may be read the State Prayers, occasional prayers and thanksgivings, or other forms of prayer. The prayers may conclude with one of the Endings (p. 107). A sermon may be preached, hymns may be sung, and the service may end with a blessing.

Evening Prayer

24 **Stand**
The minister may say

> We have come together as the family of God
>   in our Father's presence
> to offer him praise and thanksgiving,
> to hear and receive his holy word,
> to bring before him the needs of the world,
> to ask his forgiveness of our sins,
> and to seek his grace,
> that through his Son Jesus Christ
> we may give ourselves to his service.

25 A SENTENCE OF SCRIPTURE may be said (see p. 46) and
A HYMN may be sung.

26 The minister may say

> If we say we have no sin, we deceive ourselves,
> and the truth is not in us. If we confess our sins,
> God is faithful and just, and will forgive us our
> sins, and cleanse us from all unrighteousness.

or the sentences for Ash Wednesday to Lent 5 may be used.

27 The minister may say

> Let us confess our sins to almighty God.

28 **Kneel**
All   **Almighty God, our heavenly Father,**
we have sinned against you and against our
    fellow men,
in thought and word and deed,
through negligence, through weakness,
through our own deliberate fault.
We are truly sorry
and repent of all our sins.

For the sake of your Son Jesus Christ, who
　　died for us,
forgive us all that is past;
and grant that we may serve you in newness
　　of life
to the glory of your name. Amen.

29　Priest　　Almighty God,
　　　　　　　who forgives all who truly repent,
　　　　　　　have mercy upon *you*,
　　　　　　　pardon and deliver *you* from all *your* sins,
　　　　　　　confirm and strengthen *you* in all goodness,
　　　　　　　and keep *you* in life eternal;
　　　　　　　through Jesus Christ our Lord. **Amen.**

30　Instead of section 28 one of the alternative Confessions may
　　be used (pp. 165, 166).

31　**Stand**
　　Minister　　O Lord, open our lips;
　　People　　**and our mouth shall proclaim your praise.**

　　Minister　　Let us worship the Lord.
　　People　　**All praise to his name.**

　　All　　　　**Glory to the Father, and to the Son,**
　　　　　　　　and to the Holy Spirit:
　　　　　　　　as it was in the beginning, is now,
　　　　　　　　and shall be for ever. Amen.

32　PSALM 134, or O GLADSOME LIGHT,
　　or THE EASTER ANTHEMS

　　PSALM 134
1　**Come bless the Lord　all you | servants · of the | Lord:**
　　　you that by night | stand · in the | house of · our | God.

2　**Lift up your hands toward the holy place and |**
　　bless the | Lord:
　　　may the Lord bless you from Zion
　　　the | Lord who · made | heaven · and | earth.

Glory to the Father and ˈ to the ˈ Son:
   and ˈ to the ˈ Holy ˈ Spirit;
as it was in the beˈginning is ˈ now:
   and shall be for ˈ ever. ˈ A ˈ men.

O GLADSOME LIGHT

1   O gladsome light, O grace
Of God the Father's face,
The eternal splendour wearing;
Celestial, holy, blest,
Our Saviour Jesus Christ,
Joyful in thine appearing.

2   Now, ere day fadeth quite,
We see the evening light,
Our wonted hymn outpouring;
Father of might unknown,
Thee, his incarnate Son,
And Holy Spirit adoring.

3   To thee of right belongs
All praise of holy songs,
O Son of God, lifegiver;
Thee, therefore, O Most High,
The world doth glorify,
And shall exalt for ever.

Other translations of the original may be used.

THE EASTER ANTHEMS

1   Christ our passover has been ˈ sacri·ficed ˈ for us:
   so let us ˈ cele ˈ brate the ˈ feast,

2   not with the old leaven of corˈruption · and ˈ wickedness:
   but with the unleavened ˈ bread of · sin ˈ cerity · and ˈ truth.

3   Christ once raised from the dead ˈ dies no ˈ more:
   death has no ˈ more doˈminion ˈ over him.

4   In dying he died to sin ˈ once for ˈ all:
   in ˈ living · he ˈ lives to ˈ God.

5 See yourselves therefore as | dead to | sin:
   and alive to God in | Jesus | Christ our | Lord.

6 Christ has been | raised · from the | dead:
   the | firstfruits · of | those who | sleep.

7 For as by | man came | death:
   by man has come also the resur|rection | of the | dead:

8 for as in | Adam · all | die:
   even so in Christ shall | all be | made a |live.

   Glory to the Father and | to the | Son:
   and | to the | Holy | Spirit;
   as it was in the be|ginning is | now:
   and shall be for |ever. |A|men.

33 THE PSALMS appointed
   Each psalm or group of psalms ends with

   Glory to the Father and | to the | Son:
   and | to the | Holy | Spirit;
   as it was in the be|ginning is | now:
   and shall be for |ever. |A|men.

34 Sit
   THE FIRST READING, from the Old Testament

   At the end the reader may say

            This is the word of the Lord.
   All   Thanks be to God.

   Silence may be kept.

35 Stand
   MAGNIFICAT, or BLESS THE LORD

   MAGNIFICAT (The Song of Mary)
1 My soul proclaims the | greatness · of the | Lord:
   my spirit re|joices · in | God my | saviour;

2   for he has looked with favour on his | lowly | servant:
      from this day all gener|ations · will | call me |
      blessèd;

†3   the Almighty has done | great things | for me:
      and | holy | is his | name.

4   He has mercy on | those who | fear him:
      in | every | gener|ation.

5   He has shown the | strength · of his | arm:
      he has scattered the | proud in | their con|ceit.

6   He has cast down the mighty | from their | thrones:
      and has | lifted | up the | lowly.

7   He has filled the hungry with | good | things:
      and the rich he has | sent a|way | empty.

8   He has come to the help of his | servant | Israel:
      for he has re|membered · his | promise · of | mercy,

9   the promise he | made · to our | fathers:
      to Abraham | and his | children · for|ever.

Glory to the Father and | to the | Son:
      and | to the | Holy | Spirit;
as it was in the be|ginning is | now:
      and shall be for | ever. | A|men.

BLESS THE LORD

1   Bless the Lord the | God of · our | fathers:
      sing his | praise · and ex|alt him · for | ever.

2   Bless his holy and | glori·ous | name:
      sing his | praise · and ex|alt him · for | ever.

3   Bless him in his holy and | glori·ous | temple:
      sing his | praise · and ex|alt him · for | ever.

4   Bless him who be|holds the | depths:
      sing his | praise · and ex|alt him · for | ever.

5   Bless him who sits be|tween the | cherubim:
      sing his | praise · and ex|alt him · for | ever.

6 **Bless him on the | throne of · his | kingdom:**
   sing his | praise · and ex | alt him · for | ever.

7 **Bless him in the | heights of | heaven:**
   sing his | praise · and ex | alt him · for | ever.

Bless the Father the Son and the | Holy | Spirit:
   sing his | praise · and ex | alt him · for | ever.

36 **Sit**
   THE SECOND READING, from the New Testament

   At the end the reader may say

   This is the word of the Lord.
All   **Thanks be to God.**

   Silence may be kept.

37 A SERMON may be preached here, or at the end of
   the service.

38 **Stand**
   NUNC DIMITTIS, or THE SONG OF CHRIST'S GLORY,
   or GLORY AND HONOUR

   NUNC DIMITTIS (The Song of Simeon)
1 **Lord now you let your servant | go in | peace:**
   your | word has | been ful | filled.

2 **My own eyes have | seen the · sal | vation:**
   which you have prepared in the | sight of |
   every | people;

(†)3 **a light to re | veal you · to the | nations:**
   and the | glory · of your | people | Israel.

Glory to the Father and | to the | Son:
   and | to the | Holy | Spirit;
as it was in the be | ginning is | now:
   and shall be for | ever. | A | men.

THE SONG OF CHRIST'S GLORY

1 Christ Jesus was in the ˈ form of ˈ God:
   but he did not ˈ cling · to e ˈquality · with ˈ God.

2 He emptied himself * taking the ˈ form · of a ˈ servant:
   and was ˈ born · in the ˈ likeness · of ˈ men.

3 Being found in human form he ˈ humbled · him ˈself:
   and became obedient unto death ˈ even ˈ
   death · on a ˈ cross.

4 Therefore God has ˈ highly · ex ˈalted him:
   and bestowed on him the ˈ name a·bove ˈ every ˈ name,

5 that at the name of Jesus every ˈ knee should ˈ bow:
   in heaven and on ˈ earth and ˈ under · the ˈ earth;

6 and every tongue confess that Jesus ˈ Christ is ˈ Lord:
   to the ˈ glory · of ˈ God the ˈ Father.

Glory to the Father and ˈ to the ˈ Son:
   and ˈ to the ˈ Holy ˈ Spirit;
as it was in the be ˈginning is ˈ now:
   and shall be for ˈ ever. ˈ A ˈmen.

GLORY AND HONOUR

1 Glory and ˈ honour · and ˈ power:
   are yours by ˈ right O ˈ Lord our ˈ God;

2 for you cre ˈated ˈ all things:
   and by your ˈ will they ˈ have their ˈ being.

3 Glory and ˈ honour · and ˈ power:
   are yours by ˈ right O ˈ Lamb · who was ˈ slain;

4 for by your blood you ransomed ˈ men for ˈ God:
   from every race and language * from ˈ every ˈ
   people · and ˈ nation,

5 to make them a ˈ kingdom · of ˈ priests:
   to stand and ˈ serve be ˈfore our ˈ God.

To him who sits on the throne ˈ and · to the ˈ Lamb:
   be praise and honour glory and might * for ever and ˈ
   ever. ˈ A ˈmen.

All   I believe in God, the Father almighty,
                creator of heaven and earth.

                I believe in Jesus Christ, his only Son,
                    our Lord.
                He was conceived by the power of the
                    Holy Spirit
                and born of the Virgin Mary.
                He suffered under Pontius Pilate,
                was crucified, died, and was buried.
                He descended to the dead.
                On the third day he rose again.
                He ascended into heaven,
                and is seated at the right hand
                    of the Father.
                He will come again to judge the living
                    and the dead.

                I believe in the Holy Spirit,
                the holy catholic Church,
                the communion of saints,
                the forgiveness of sins,
                the resurrection of the body,
                and the life everlasting. Amen.

40 **Kneel**
The minister may say

            Lord, have mercy upon us.
People **Christ, have mercy upon us.**
Minister   Lord, have mercy upon us.

41 **All**

Our Father in heaven,   or   Our Father, who art in heaven,
hallowed be your name,   hallowed be thy name;
your kingdom come,   thy kingdom come;
your will be done,   thy will be done;
on earth as in heaven.   on earth as it is in heaven.
Give us today our daily bread.   Give us this day our daily bread.
Forgive us our sins   And forgive us our trespasses,
as we forgive those   as we forgive those
    who sin against us.   who trespass against us.

Lead us not into temptation
but deliver us from evil.

For the kingdom, the power,
and the glory are yours
now and for ever. Amen.

And lead us not into temptation;
but deliver us from evil.

For thine is the kingdom,
the power, and the glory,
for ever and ever. Amen.

42   These versicles and responses may be said.

Minister   Show us your mercy, O Lord;
People   and grant us your salvation.

Minister   O Lord, save the Queen;
People   and teach her counsellors wisdom.

Minister   Let your priests be clothed with righteousness;
People   and let your servants shout for joy.

Minister   O Lord, make your ways known upon the earth;
People   let all nations acknowledge your saving power.

Minister   Give your people the blessing of peace;
People   and let your glory be over all the world.

Minister   Make our hearts clean, O God;
People   and renew a right spirit within us.

43   THE COLLECT OF THE DAY

44   THIS COLLECT may be said.

O God,
the source of all good desires,
all right judgements, and all just works:
give to your servants that peace
    which the world cannot give;
that our hearts may be set to obey
    your commandments,
and that freed from fear of our enemies,
we may pass our time in rest and quietness;
through Jesus Christ our Lord. **Amen.**

45   THIS COLLECT is said.

> Lighten our darkness,
> Lord, we pray;
> and in your mercy defend us
> from all perils and dangers of this night;
> for the love of your only Son,
> our Saviour Jesus Christ. **Amen.**

46   Here may be read the State Prayers, occasional prayers and thanksgivings, or other forms of prayer. The prayers may conclude with one of the Endings (p. 107). A sermon may be preached, hymns may be sung, and the service may end with a blessing.

Prayers for Various Occasions

1   THE LITANY

Sections I and VI must always be used, but a selection of appropriate suffrages may be made from Sections II, III, IV and V.

I

Let us pray.

God the Father,
have mercy on us.

God the Son,
have mercy on us.

God the Holy Spirit,
have mercy on us.

Holy, blessed, and glorious Trinity,
have mercy on us.

II

From all evil and mischief;
from pride, vanity, and hypocrisy;
from envy, hatred, and malice;
and from all evil intent,
Good Lord, deliver us.

From sloth, worldliness, and love of money;
from hardness of heart
and contempt for your word and your laws,
Good Lord, deliver us.

From sins of body and mind;
from the deceits of the world, the flesh,
    and the devil,
Good Lord, deliver us.

From famine and disaster;
from violence, murder, and dying unprepared,
Good Lord, deliver us.

In all times of sorrow;
in all times of joy;
in the hour of death,
and at the day of judgement,
Good Lord, deliver us.

By the mystery of your holy incarnation;
by your birth, childhood, and obedience;
by your baptism, fasting, and temptation,
Good Lord, deliver us.

By your ministry in word and work;
by your mighty acts of power;
and by your preaching of the kingdom,
Good Lord, deliver us.

By your agony and trial;
by your cross and passion;
and by your precious death and burial,
Good Lord, deliver us.

By your mighty resurrection;
by your glorious ascension;
and by your sending of the Holy Spirit,
Good Lord, deliver us.

III

Hear our prayers, O Lord our God.
Hear us, good Lord.

Govern and direct your holy Church; fill it with
love and truth; and grant it that unity which is
your will.
Hear us, good Lord.

Give us boldness to preach the gospel in all the
world, and to make disciples of all the nations.
Hear us, good Lord.

Enlighten your ministers with knowledge and
understanding, that by their teaching and their
lives they may proclaim your word.
Hear us, good Lord.

Give your people grace to hear and receive your word, and to bring forth the fruit of the Spirit.
Hear us, good Lord.

Bring into the way of truth all who have erred and are deceived.
Hear us, good Lord.

Strengthen those who stand; comfort and help the fainthearted; raise up the fallen; and finally beat down Satan under our feet.
Hear us, good Lord.

IV

Guide the leaders of the nations into the ways of peace and justice.
Hear us, good Lord.

Guard and strengthen your servant Elizabeth our Queen, that she may put her trust in you, and seek your honour and glory.
Hear us, good Lord.

Endue the High Court of Parliament and all the Ministers of the Crown with wisdom and understanding.
Hear us, good Lord.

Bless those who administer the law, that they may uphold justice, honesty, and truth.
Hear us, good Lord.

Teach us to use the fruits of the earth to your glory, and for the good of all mankind.
Hear us, good Lord.

Bless and keep all your people.
Hear us, good Lord.

V

Help and comfort the lonely, the bereaved, and the oppressed.
Lord, have mercy.

Keep in safety those who travel, and all who are in danger.
Lord, have mercy.

Heal the sick in body and mind, and provide for the homeless, the hungry, and the destitute.
Lord, have mercy.

Show your pity on prisoners and refugees, and all who are in trouble.
Lord, have mercy.

Forgive our enemies, persecutors, and slanderers, and turn their hearts.
Lord, have mercy.

Hear us as we remember those who have died in the peace of Christ, both those who have confessed the faith and those whose faith is known to you alone, and grant us with them a share in your eternal kingdom.
Lord, have mercy.

VI

Give us true repentance;
forgive us our sins of negligence and ignorance and our deliberate sins;
and grant us the grace of your Holy Spirit
to amend our lives according to your holy word.
**Holy God,
holy and strong,
holy and immortal,
have mercy upon us.**

One of the prayers (sections 13 and 14), and the Lord's Prayer may be added.
When the Litany is said instead of the Prayers at Morning or Evening Prayer, the Lord's Prayer, the Collect of the Day, and the Grace are added here.

STATE PRAYERS

2   Almighty God, the fountain of all goodness,
bless our Sovereign Lady, Queen Elizabeth, and
all who are in authority under her; that they may
order all things in wisdom and equity,
righteousness and peace, to the honour of your
name, and the good of your Church and people;
through Jesus Christ our Lord. **Amen.**

3   Almighty God, the fountain of all goodness,
bless, we pray, Elizabeth the Queen Mother,
Philip Duke of Edinburgh, the Prince and
Princess of Wales, and all the Royal Family.
Endue them with your Holy Spirit; enrich them
with your heavenly grace; prosper them with all
happiness; and bring them to your everlasting
kingdom; through Jesus Christ our Lord. **Amen.**

4   Almighty and everlasting God, the only worker
of great marvels, send down upon our bishops
and other pastors and all congregations
committed to their care the spirit of your saving
grace; and that they may truly please you, pour
upon them the continual dew of your blessing.
Grant this, O Lord, for the honour of our
advocate and mediator, Jesus Christ. **Amen.**

A GENERAL INTERCESSION

5   O God, the creator and preserver of all
mankind, we pray for men of every race, and in
every kind of need: make your ways known on
earth, your saving power among all nations.
(Especially we pray for . . .)
Lord, in your mercy
hear our prayer.

We pray for your Church throughout the world:
guide and govern us by your Holy Spirit, that
all who profess and call themselves Christians

may be led into the way of truth, and hold the
faith in unity of spirit, in the bond of peace, and
in righteousness of life. (Especially we pray for . . .)
Lord, in your mercy
hear our prayer.

We commend to your fatherly goodness all who
are anxious or distressed in mind or body;
comfort and relieve them in their need; give them
patience in their sufferings, and bring good
out of their troubles. (Especially we pray for . . .)
Merciful Father,
accept these prayers
for the sake of your Son,
our Saviour Jesus Christ. Amen.

A GENERAL THANKSGIVING

6

Almighty God, Father of all mercies,
we your unworthy servants give you most
    humble and hearty thanks
for all your goodness and loving kindness
to us and to all men.
We bless you for our creation, preservation,
    and all the blessings of this life;
but above all for your immeasurable love
in the redemption of the world by our
    Lord Jesus Christ,
for the means of grace, and for the hope of glory.
And give us, we pray, such a sense of all
    your mercies
that our hearts may be unfeignedly thankful,
and that we show forth your praise,
not only with our lips but in our lives,
by giving up ourselves to your service,
and by walking before you in holiness
    and righteousness all our days;
through Jesus Christ our Lord,
to whom, with you and the Holy Spirit,
    be all honour and glory,
for ever and ever. Amen.

A PRAYER OF DEDICATION

7   This may be used at the end of Morning or Evening Prayer, or at a service of Ante-Communion.

> **Almighty God,**
> **we thank you for the gift of your holy word.**
> **May it be a lantern to our feet,**
> **a light to our paths,**
> **and a strength to our lives.**
> **Take us and use us**
> **to love and serve all men**
> **in the power of the Holy Spirit**
> **and in the name of your Son,**
> **Jesus Christ our Lord. Amen.**

CONCLUDING PRAYERS

8   Almighty God, you have given us grace at this time with one accord to make our common supplication to you; and you have promised that when two or three are gathered together in your name you will grant their requests. Fulfil now, O Lord, the desires and petitions of your servants, as may be most expedient for them, granting us in this world knowledge of your truth, and in the world to come, life everlasting. **Amen.**

9   Heavenly Father, you have promised through your Son Jesus Christ, that when we meet in his name, and pray according to his mind, he will be among us and will hear our prayer. In your love and wisdom fulfil our desires, and give us your greatest gift, which is to know you, the only true God, and Jesus Christ our Lord; who is alive and reigns with you and the Holy Spirit, one God, now and for ever. **Amen.**

10   Be with us, Lord, in all our prayers, and direct our way toward the attainment of salvation; that among the changes and chances of this mortal life, we may always be defended by your gracious help; through Jesus Christ our Lord. **Amen.**

11   Almighty and eternal God, sanctify and govern our hearts and bodies in the ways of your laws and the works of your commandments; that under your protection, now and ever, we may be preserved in body and soul; through Jesus Christ our Lord. **Amen.**

12   Guide us, Lord, in all our doings with your gracious favour, and further us with your continual help; that in all our works begun, continued, and ended in you, we may glorify your holy name, and by your mercy attain everlasting life; through Jesus Christ our Lord. **Amen.**

13   Almighty God, the fountain of all wisdom, you know our needs before we ask, and our ignorance in asking; have compassion on our weakness, and give us those things which for our unworthiness we dare not, and for our blindness we cannot ask, for the sake of your Son, Jesus Christ our Lord. **Amen.**

14   Almighty God, you have promised to hear the prayers of those who ask in your Son's name; we pray that what we have asked faithfully we may obtain effectually; through Jesus Christ our Lord. **Amen.**

ENDINGS

15

The grace of our Lord Jesus Christ, and the love of God, and the fellowship of the Holy Spirit be with us all evermore. **Amen.**

16

Now to him who is able to do immeasurably more than all we can ask or conceive, by the power which is at work among us, to him be glory in the Church and in Christ Jesus throughout all ages. **Amen.**

17

The Lord be with you
and also with you.

Let us bless the Lord.
Thanks be to God.

BLESSINGS

18

The Lord bless you and watch over you,
the Lord make his face shine upon you
and be gracious to you,
the Lord look kindly on you
   and give you peace;
and the blessing of God almighty,
the Father, the Son, and the Holy Spirit,
be among you and remain with you always.
Amen.

19

The love of the Lord Jesus
draw you to himself,
the power of the Lord Jesus
strengthen you in his service,
the joy of the Lord Jesus fill your hearts;
and the blessing of God almighty,
the Father, the Son, and the Holy Spirit,
be among you and remain with you always.
Amen.

The Order for Holy Communion

also called The Eucharist

and The Lord's Supper

Rite A

NOTES

1 **Preparation** Careful devotional preparation before the service is recommended for every communicant.

2 **The President** The president (who, in accordance with the provisions of Canon B12 'Of the ministry of the Holy Communion', must have been episcopally ordained priest) presides over the whole service. He says the opening Greeting, the Collect, the Absolution, the Peace, and the Blessing; he himself must take the bread and the cup before replacing them on the holy table, say the Eucharistic Prayer, break the consecrated bread, and receive the sacrament on every occasion. The remaining parts of the service he may delegate to others. When necessity dictates, a deacon or lay person may preside over the Ministry of the Word.

When the Bishop is present, it is appropriate that he should act as president. He may also delegate sections 32-49 to a priest.

3 **Posture** When a certain posture is particularly appropriate, it is indicated in the margin. For the rest of the service local custom may be established and followed. The Eucharistic Prayer (sections 38, 39, 40, and 41) is a single prayer, the unity of which may be obscured by changes of posture in the course of it.

4 **Seasonal Material** The seasonal sentences and blessings are optional. Any other appropriate scriptural sentences may be read at sections 1 and 50 at the discretion of the president and 'Alleluia' may be added to any sentence from Easter Day until Pentecost.

5 **Greetings** (section 2 etc.) In addition to the points where greetings are provided, at other suitable points (e.g. before the Gospel and before the Blessing and Dismissal) the minister may say 'The Lord be with you' and the congregation reply 'and also with you'.

6   **Prayers of Penitence** These are used either after section 4 or section 23 (but see Note 22 below for occasions when the Order following the pattern of the Book of Common Prayer is used).

7   **Kyrie eleison** (section 9) This may be used in English or Greek. Alternative versions are set out in section 79.

8   **Gloria in excelsis** (sections 10 and 73) This canticle may be appropriately omitted during Advent and Lent, and on weekdays which are not Principal or Greater Holy Days. It may also be used at sections 1 and 16.

9   **The Collect** (section 11) The Collect may be introduced by the words 'Let us pray' and a brief bidding, after which silence may be kept.

10   **Readings** Where one of the three readings is to be omitted, provision for this is found in Table 3A, I pp. 1049–60. See p. 981, note 2.

11   **The Gospel in Holy Week** (section 17) From Palm Sunday to the Wednesday in Holy Week, and on Good Friday, the Passion Gospel may be introduced: 'The Passion of our Lord Jesus Christ according to N', and concluded: 'This is the Passion of the Lord'. No responses are used.

12   **The Sermon** (section 18) The sermon is an integral part of the Ministry of the Word. A sermon should normally be preached at all celebrations on Sundays and other Holy Days.

13   **Proper Prefaces** The Proper Prefaces are set out in section 76. They are obligatory when this is indicated in the seasonal propers but may be used on other suitable occasions. The Sunday Prefaces (31), (32), and (33) are for use with the Fourth Eucharistic Prayer and the Order following the pattern of the Book of Common Prayer.

14 **Second Eucharistic Prayer** (section 39) The three paragraphs beginning 'For he is your living Word' and ending 'a people for your own possession' may be omitted if a Proper Preface is used.

15 **Acclamations** These are optional. They may be introduced by the president with the words 'Let us proclaim the mystery of faith' or with other suitable words or they may be used without introduction.

16 **Manual Acts** In addition to the taking of the bread and the cup at section 36 the president may use traditional manual acts during the Eucharistic Prayers.

17 **Words of Invitation** (section 45) The words provided are to be used at least on Sundays and other Holy Days, and those in section 85 may be added. On other days those in section 85 may be substituted.

18 **The Blessing** (section 54) In addition to the blessings provided here and in section 77 the president may at his discretion use others.

19 **Notices** Banns of marriage and other notices may be published after section 2, section 19, or section 53.

20 **Hymns, Canticles, the Peace, the Collection and Presentation of the Offerings of the People, and the Preparation of the Gifts of Bread and Wine** Points are indicated for these, but if occasion requires they may occur elsewhere.

21 **Silence** After sections 6, 13, 15, 17, 18, 26, before sections 42 and 51, and after the biddings in section 21, silence may be kept.

22 **The Order following the pattern of the Book of Common Prayer** (sections 22 and 57-75) When this Order is being followed the Prayers of Penitence should not be used at section 4, as they are requisite at section 59. The Order provided should then be followed in its entirety.

23 **Ministry to the Sick** When Holy Communion is ministered to the sick, the Laying on of Hands or Anointing may follow the Absolution (section 28); the alternative Eucharistic Prayer for use with the sick (section 84) may be used; and the service may be shortened if the needs of the patient require it.

24 **A Service without Communion** When there is no communion, the minister reads the service as far as the Absolution (section 28), and then adds the Lord's Prayer, the General Thanksgiving, and/or other prayers (see section 86) at his discretion, ending with the Grace. When such a service is led by a deacon or lay person, 'us' is said instead of 'you' in the Absolution.

The Order for
Holy Communion
Rite A

THE PREPARATION

1   At the entry of the ministers AN APPROPRIATE
SENTENCE may be used; and A HYMN, A CANTICLE,
or A PSALM may be sung.

2   The president welcomes the people using these or other
appropriate words.

> The Lord be with you or The Lord is here.
>
> **All**   **and also with you.**   **His Spirit is with us.**

or Easter Day to Pentecost

> Alleluia! Christ is risen.
>
> **All**   **He is risen indeed. Alleluia!**

3   This prayer may be said.

> **All**   **Almighty God,**
> **to whom all hearts are open,**
> **all desires known,**
> **and from whom no secrets are hidden:**
> **cleanse the thoughts of our hearts**
> **by the inspiration of your Holy Spirit,**
> **that we may perfectly love you,**
> **and worthily magnify your holy name;**
> **through Christ our Lord. Amen.**

PRAYERS OF PENITENCE

4   THE PRAYERS OF PENITENCE (sections 5-8) may be said
     here, or after section 23; if they are said here, sections 6-8 are
     always used.
     Alternative confessions may be used (see section 80).

5   THE COMMANDMENTS (section 78) or the following
     SUMMARY OF THE LAW may be said.

   Minister   Our Lord Jesus Christ said: The first
               commandment is this: 'Hear, O Israel, the Lord
               our God is the only Lord. You shall love the Lord
               your God with all your heart, with all your soul,
               with all your mind, and with all your strength.'
               The second is this: 'Love your neighbour as
               yourself.' There is no other commandment
               greater than these.
   All   Amen. Lord, have mercy.

6   The minister invites the congregation to confess their sins in
     these or other suitable words (see section 25).

               God so loved the world that he gave his only
               Son Jesus Christ to save us from our sins, to be
               our advocate in heaven, and to bring us to
               eternal life.

               Let us confess our sins, in penitence and faith,
               firmly resolved to keep God's commandments
               and to live in love and peace with all men.

7   All   Almighty God, our heavenly Father,
               we have sinned against you and against our
                   fellow men,
               in thought and word and deed,
               through negligence, through weakness,
               through our own deliberate fault.
               We are truly sorry
               and repent of all our sins.

For the sake of your Son Jesus Christ, who
    died for us,
forgive us all that is past;
and grant that we may serve you in newness
    of life
to the glory of your name. Amen.

8   President   Almighty God,
who forgives all who truly repent,
have mercy upon *you*,
pardon and deliver *you* from all *your* sins,
confirm and strengthen *you* in all goodness,
and keep *you* in life eternal;
through Jesus Christ our Lord. **Amen.**

---

9   KYRIE ELEISON may be said (see also section 79).

Lord, have mercy.
Lord, have mercy.

Christ, have mercy.
Christ, have mercy.

Lord, have mercy.
Lord, have mercy.

10   GLORIA IN EXCELSIS may be said.

All   **Glory to God in the highest,**
and peace to his people on earth.

Lord God, heavenly King,
almighty God and Father,
we worship you, we give you thanks,
we praise you for your glory.

Lord Jesus Christ, only Son of the Father,
Lord God, Lamb of God,
you take away the sin of the world:
have mercy on us;
you are seated at the right hand of the Father:
receive our prayer.

For you alone are the Holy One,
you alone are the Lord,
you alone are the Most High,
Jesus Christ,
with the Holy Spirit,
in the glory of God the Father. Amen.

11   The president says THE COLLECT.

THE MINISTRY OF THE WORD

12   Either two or three readings from scripture follow, the last of
which is always the Gospel.

13   **Sit**
OLD TESTAMENT READING

At the end the reader may say

            This is the word of the Lord.
All   **Thanks be to God.**

14   A PSALM may be used.

15   **Sit**
NEW TESTAMENT READING (EPISTLE)

At the end the reader may say

            This is the word of the Lord.
All   **Thanks be to God.**

16   A CANTICLE, A HYMN, or A PSALM may be used.

17 **Stand**
THE GOSPEL. When it is announced

All   **Glory to Christ our Saviour.**

At the end the reader says

          This is the Gospel of Christ.
All   **Praise to Christ our Lord.**

18 **Sit**
THE SERMON

19 **Stand**
THE NICENE CREED is said on Sundays and other Holy
Days, and may be said on other days.

All   **We believe in one God,**
          the Father, the almighty,
          maker of heaven and earth,
          of all that is,
          seen and unseen.

          We believe in one Lord, Jesus Christ,
          the only Son of God,
          eternally begotten of the Father,
          God from God, Light from Light,
          true God from true God,
          begotten, not made,
          of one Being with the Father.
          Through him all things were made.
          For us men and for our salvation
          he came down from heaven;
          by the power of the Holy Spirit
          he became incarnate of the Virgin Mary,
          and was made man.
          For our sake he was crucified under
          Pontius Pilate;
          he suffered death and was buried.

On the third day he rose again
in accordance with the Scriptures;
he ascended into heaven
and is seated at the right hand of the Father.
He will come again in glory
to judge the living and the dead,
and his kingdom will have no end.

We believe in the Holy Spirit,
the Lord, the giver of life,
who proceeds from the Father and the Son.
With the Father and the Son he is worshipped
and glorified.
He has spoken through the Prophets.

We believe in one holy catholic
and apostolic Church.
We acknowledge one baptism for the
forgiveness of sins.
We look for the resurrection of the dead,
and the life of the world to come. Amen.

THE INTERCESSION

20 INTERCESSIONS AND THANKSGIVINGS are led by the president, or by others. The form below, or one of those in section 81, or other suitable words, may be used.

21 This form may be used
(a) with the insertion of specific subjects between the paragraphs;
(b) as a continuous whole with or without brief biddings.

Not all paragraphs need be used on every occasion.
Individual names may be added at the places indicated.
This response may be used before or after each paragraph.

Minister   Lord, in your mercy
All   **hear our prayer.**

Let us pray for the Church and for the world,
and let us thank God for his goodness.

Almighty God, our heavenly Father, you
promised through your Son Jesus Christ to hear
us when we pray in faith.

Strengthen N our bishop and all your Church in
the service of Christ; that those who confess your
name may be united in your truth, live together
in your love, and reveal your glory in the world.

Bless and guide Elizabeth our Queen; give
wisdom to all in authority; and direct this and
every nation in the ways of justice and of peace;
that men may honour one another, and seek the
common good.

Give grace to us, our families and friends, and to
all our neighbours; that we may serve Christ in
one another, and love as he loves us.

Comfort and heal all those who suffer in body,
mind, or spirit . . .; give them courage and hope
in their troubles; and bring them the joy of your
salvation.

Hear us as we remember those who have died in
the faith of Christ . . .; according to your
promises, grant us with them a share in your
eternal kingdom.

Rejoicing in the fellowship of (N and of) all your
saints, we commend ourselves and all Christian
people to your unfailing love.

All   Merciful Father,
**accept these prayers
for the sake of your Son,
our Saviour Jesus Christ. Amen.**

22   The Order following the pattern of the Book of Common
Prayer continues at section 57.

PRAYERS OF PENITENCE

23 THE PRAYERS OF PENITENCE (sections 24-28) are said here, if they have not been said after section 4; if they are said here, sections 26-28 are always used.
Alternative confessions may be used (see section 80).

24 THE COMMANDMENTS (section 78) or the following SUMMARY OF THE LAW may be said.

Minister   Our Lord Jesus Christ said: The first commandment is this: 'Hear, O Israel, the Lord our God is the only Lord. You shall love the Lord your God with all your heart, with all your soul, with all your mind, and with all your strength.' The second is this: 'Love your neighbour as yourself.' There is no other commandment greater than these.

All   **Amen. Lord, have mercy.**

25 The minister may say

God so loved the world that he gave his only Son Jesus Christ to save us from our sins, to be our advocate in heaven, and to bring us to eternal life.

or one or more of these SENTENCES.

Hear the words of comfort our Saviour Christ says to all who truly turn to him:
Come to me, all who labour and are heavy laden, and I will give you rest. *Matthew 11.28*

God so loved the world that he gave his only Son, that whoever believes in him should not perish but have eternal life. *John 3.16*

Hear what Saint Paul says:
This saying is true and worthy of full
acceptance, that Christ Jesus came into the
world to save sinners. *1 Timothy 1.15*

Hear what Saint John says:
If anyone sins, we have an advocate with the
Father, Jesus Christ the righteous; and he
is the propitiation for our sins. *1 John 2.1*

26   Minister   Let us confess our sins, in penitence and faith,
firmly resolved to keep God's commandments
and to live in love and peace with all men.

27   **All**   **Almighty God, our heavenly Father,**
we have sinned against you and against our
fellow men,
in thought and word and deed,
through negligence, through weakness,
through our own deliberate fault.
We are truly sorry
and repent of all our sins.
For the sake of your Son Jesus Christ, who
died for us,
forgive us all that is past;
and grant that we may serve you in newness
of life
to the glory of your name. Amen.

28   President   Almighty God,
who forgives all who truly repent,
have mercy upon *you*,
pardon and deliver *you* from all *your* sins,
confirm and strengthen *you* in all goodness,
and keep *you* in life eternal;
through Jesus Christ our Lord. **Amen.**

> We do not presume
> to come to this your table, merciful Lord,
> trusting in our own righteousness,
> but in your manifold and great mercies.
> We are not worthy
> so much as to gather up the crumbs under
>   your table.
> But you are the same Lord
> whose nature is always to have mercy.
> Grant us therefore, gracious Lord,
> so to eat the flesh of your dear Son
>   Jesus Christ
> and to drink his blood,
> that we may evermore dwell in him
> and he in us. Amen.

The alternative prayer at section 82 may be used.

THE MINISTRY OF THE SACRAMENT

THE PEACE

30 **Stand**
The president says either of the following or other suitable words (see section 83).

> Christ is our peace.
> He has reconciled us to God
>   in one body by the cross.
> We meet in his name and share his peace.

or
> We are the Body of Christ.
> In the one Spirit we were all baptized into
>   one body.
> Let us then pursue all that makes for peace
> and builds up our common life.

He then says

> The peace of the Lord be always with you
>
> **All**   **and also with you.**

31 The president may say

> Let us offer one another a sign of peace.

and all may exchange a sign of peace.

THE PREPARATION OF THE GIFTS

32 The bread and wine are placed on the holy table.

33 The president may praise God for his gifts in appropriate
words to which all respond

> **Blessed be God for ever.**

34 The offerings of the people may be collected and presented.
These words may be used.

> **Yours, Lord, is the greatness, the power,**
> **the glory, the splendour, and the majesty;**
> **for everything in heaven and on earth is yours.**
> **All things come from you,**
> **and of your own do we give you.**

35 At the preparation of the gifts A HYMN may be sung.

THE EUCHARISTIC PRAYER

THE TAKING OF THE BREAD AND CUP AND THE GIVING OF THANKS

36   The president takes the bread and cup into his hands and replaces them on the holy table.

37   The president uses one of the four EUCHARISTIC PRAYERS which follow.

---

38   **FIRST EUCHARISTIC PRAYER**

President   The Lord be with you or The Lord is here.
All   **and also with you.   His Spirit is with us.**

President   Lift up your hearts.
All   **We lift them to the Lord.**

President   Let us give thanks to the Lord our God.
All   **It is right to give him thanks and praise.**

President   It is indeed right,
it is our duty and our joy,
at all times and in all places
to give you thanks and praise,
holy Father, heavenly King,
almighty and eternal God,
through Jesus Christ your only Son our Lord.

For he is your living Word;
through him you have created all things from
    the beginning,
and formed us in your own image.

Through him you have freed us from the
    slavery of sin,
giving him to be born as man and to die upon
    the cross;
you raised him from the dead
and exalted him to your right hand on high.

Through him you have sent upon us
your holy and life-giving Spirit,
and made us a people for your own possession.

PROPER PREFACE, when appropriate (section 76)

Therefore with angels and archangels,
and with all the company of heaven,
we proclaim your great and glorious name,
for ever praising you and saying:

All **Holy, holy, holy Lord,**
God of power and might,
heaven and earth are full of your glory.
Hosanna in the highest.

This ANTHEM may also be used.

Blessed is he who comes in the name of the Lord.
Hosanna in the highest.

President Accept our praises, heavenly Father,
through your Son our Saviour Jesus Christ;
and as we follow his example and obey
    his command,
grant that by the power of your Holy Spirit
these gifts of bread and wine
may be to us his body and his blood;

Who in the same night that he was betrayed,
took bread and gave you thanks;
he broke it and gave it to his disciples,
    saying,
Take, eat; this is my body which is given
    for you;
do this in remembrance of me.
In the same way, after supper
he took the cup and gave you thanks;
he gave it to them, saying,
Drink this, all of you;
this is my blood of the new covenant,
which is shed for you and for many for the
    forgiveness of sins.
Do this, as often as you drink it,

in remembrance of me.

All **Christ has died:**
Christ is risen:
Christ will come again.

President Therefore, heavenly Father,
we remember his offering of himself
made once for all upon the cross,
and proclaim his mighty resurrection and
glorious ascension.
As we look for his coming in glory,
we celebrate with this bread and this cup
his one perfect sacrifice.

Accept through him, our great high priest,
this our sacrifice of thanks and praise;
and as we eat and drink these holy gifts
in the presence of your divine majesty,
renew us by your Spirit,
inspire us with your love,
and unite us in the body of your Son,
Jesus Christ our Lord.

Through him, and with him, and in him,
by the power of the Holy Spirit,
with all who stand before you in earth
and heaven,
we worship you, Father almighty,
in songs of everlasting praise:

All **Blessing and honour and glory and power**
be yours for ever and ever. Amen.

Silence may be kept.

The service continues with THE LORD'S PRAYER at section
42 on p. 142.

President   The Lord be with you or The Lord is here.
All   **and also with you.   His Spirit is with us.**

President   Lift up your hearts.
All   **We lift them to the Lord.**

President   Let us give thanks to the Lord our God.
All   **It is right to give him thanks and praise.**

President   It is indeed right,
            it is our duty and our joy,
            at all times and in all places
            to give you thanks and praise,
            holy Father, heavenly King,
            almighty and eternal God,
            through Jesus Christ your only Son our Lord.

The following may be omitted if a Proper Preface is used.

            For he is your living Word;
            through him you have created all things from
                the beginning,
            and formed us in your own image.

            Through him you have freed us from the
                slavery of sin,
            giving him to be born as man and to die upon
                the cross;
            you raised him from the dead
            and exalted him to your right hand on high.

            Through him you have sent upon us
            your holy and life-giving Spirit,
            and made us a people for your own possession.

PROPER PREFACE, when appropriate (section 76)

            Therefore with angels and archangels,
            and with all the company of heaven,
            we proclaim your great and glorious name,
            for ever praising you and saying:

All   Holy, holy, holy Lord,
God of power and might,
heaven and earth are full of your glory.
Hosanna in the highest.

This ANTHEM may also be used.

Blessed is he who comes in the name of
the Lord.
Hosanna in the highest.

President   Hear us, heavenly Father,
through Jesus Christ your Son our Lord,
through him accept our sacrifice of praise;
and grant that by the power of your
Holy Spirit
these gifts of bread and wine
may be to us his body and his blood;

Who in the same night that he was betrayed,
took bread and gave you thanks;
he broke it and gave it to his disciples,
saying,
Take, eat; this is my body which is given
for you;
do this in remembrance of me.
In the same way, after supper
he took the cup and gave you thanks;
he gave it to them, saying,
Drink this, all of you;
this is my blood of the new covenant,
which is shed for you and for many for the
forgiveness of sins.
Do this, as often as you drink it,
in remembrance of me.

All   Christ has died:
Christ is risen:
Christ will come again.

President Therefore, Lord and heavenly Father,
having in remembrance his death once for all
    upon the cross,
his resurrection from the dead,
and his ascension into heaven,
and looking for the coming of his kingdom,
we make with this bread and this cup
the memorial of Christ your Son our Lord.

Accept through him this offering of our duty
    and service;
and as we eat and drink these holy gifts
in the presence of your divine majesty,
fill us with your grace and heavenly blessing;
nourish us with the body and blood of your Son,
that we may grow into his likeness
and, made one by your Spirit,
become a living temple to your glory.

Through Jesus Christ our Lord,
by whom, and with whom, and in whom,
in the unity of the Holy Spirit,
all honour and glory be yours, almighty Father,
from all who stand before you in earth
    and heaven,
now and for ever. **Amen.**

Silence may be kept.

The service continues with THE LORD'S PRAYER at section 42 on p. 142.

President The Lord be with you or The Lord is here.
All   **and also with you.   His Spirit is with us.**

President Lift up your hearts.
All   **We lift them to the Lord.**

President Let us give thanks to the Lord our God.
All   **It is right to give him thanks and praise.**

President Father, we give you thanks and praise
           through your beloved Son Jesus Christ,
           your living Word through whom you have
               created all things;

           Who was sent by you, in your great goodness,
               to be our Saviour;
           by the power of the Holy Spirit he took flesh
           and, as your Son, born of the blessed Virgin,
           was seen on earth
           and went about among us;

           He opened wide his arms for us on the cross;
           he put an end to death by dying for us
           and revealed the resurrection by rising to
               new life;
           so he fulfilled your will and won for you a
               holy people.

PROPER PREFACE, when appropriate (section 76)

           Therefore with angels and archangels,
           and with all the company of heaven,
           we proclaim your great and glorious name,
           for ever praising you and saying:

All   **Holy, holy, holy Lord,**
           God of power and might,
           heaven and earth are full of your glory.
           Hosanna in the highest.

This ANTHEM may also be used.

> **Blessed is he who comes in the name of
> the Lord.
> Hosanna in the highest.**

President   Lord, you are holy indeed, the source of
all holiness;
grant that, by the power of your Holy Spirit,
and according to your holy will,
these your gifts of bread and wine
may be to us the body and blood of our Lord
Jesus Christ;

Who in the same night that he was betrayed,
took bread and gave you thanks;
he broke it and gave it to his disciples,
saying,
Take, eat; this is my body which is given
for you;
do this in remembrance of me.
In the same way, after supper
he took the cup and gave you thanks;
he gave it to them, saying,
Drink this, all of you;
this is my blood of the new covenant,
which is shed for you and for many for the
forgiveness of sins.
Do this, as often as you drink it,
in remembrance of me.

All   **Christ has died:
Christ is risen:
Christ will come again.**

President   And so, Father, calling to mind his death on
the cross,
his perfect sacrifice made once for the sins
of all men,
rejoicing at his mighty resurrection and
glorious ascension,
and looking for his coming in glory,
we celebrate this memorial of our redemption;

We thank you for counting us worthy
to stand in your presence and serve you;
we bring before you this bread and this cup;

We pray you to accept this our duty
    and service,
a spiritual sacrifice of praise and
    thanksgiving;

Send the Holy Spirit on your people
and gather into one in your kingdom
all who share this one bread and one cup,
so that we, in the company of all the saints,
may praise and glorify you for ever,
through him from whom all good things come,
Jesus Christ our Lord;

By whom, and with whom, and in whom,
in the unity of the Holy Spirit,
all honour and glory be yours, almighty Father,
for ever and ever. **Amen.**

Silence may be kept.

The service continues with THE LORD'S PRAYER at section
42 on p. 142.

41   FOURTH EUCHARISTIC PRAYER

President   The Lord be with you or The Lord is here.
All   and also with you.   His Spirit is with us.

President   Lift up your hearts.
All   We lift them to the Lord.

President   Let us give thanks to the Lord our God.
All   It is right to give him thanks and praise.

President   It is indeed right,
             it is our duty and our joy,
             at all times and in all places
             to give you thanks and praise,
             holy Father, heavenly King,
             almighty and eternal God,
             creator of heaven and earth,
             through Jesus Christ our Lord:

PROPER PREFACE, when appropriate (section 76)

The following is used when no Proper Preface is provided.

             For he is the true high priest,
             who has loosed us from our sins
             and has made us to be a royal priesthood
                 to you,
             our God and Father.

             Therefore with angels and archangels,
             and with all the company of heaven,
             we proclaim your great and glorious name,
             for ever praising you and saying:

**All   Holy, holy, holy Lord,
             God of power and might,
             heaven and earth are full of your glory.
             Hosanna in the highest.**

This ANTHEM may also be used.

**Blessed is he who comes in the name of
the Lord.
Hosanna in the highest.**

President All glory to you, our heavenly Father:
in your tender mercy
you gave your only Son Jesus Christ
to suffer death upon the cross for
    our redemption;
he made there
a full atonement for the sins of the
    whole world,
offering once for all his one sacrifice
    of himself;
he instituted,
and in his holy gospel commanded us
    to continue,
a perpetual memory of his precious death
until he comes again.

Hear us, merciful Father, we humbly pray,
and grant that by the power of your
    Holy Spirit
we who receive these gifts of your creation,
this bread and this wine,
according to your Son our Saviour Jesus
    Christ's holy institution,
in remembrance of the death that he suffered,
may be partakers of his most blessed body
    and blood;

Who in the same night that he was betrayed,
took bread and gave you thanks;
he broke it and gave it to his disciples,
    saying,
Take, eat; this is my body which is given
    for you;
do this in remembrance of me.
In the same way, after supper
he took the cup and gave you thanks;
he gave it to them, saying,

Drink this, all of you;
this is my blood of the new covenant,
which is shed for you and for many for the
    forgiveness of sins.
Do this, as often as you drink it,
in remembrance of me.

All   **Christ has died:**
Christ is risen:
Christ will come again.

President   Therefore, Lord and heavenly Father,
in remembrance of the precious death
    and passion,
the mighty resurrection and glorious ascension
of your dear Son Jesus Christ,
we offer you through him this sacrifice of
    praise and thanksgiving.

Grant that by his merits and death,
and through faith in his blood,
we and all your Church may receive forgiveness
    of our sins
and all other benefits of his passion.
Although we are unworthy, through our
    many sins,
to offer you any sacrifice,
yet we pray that you will accept this,
the duty and service that we owe;
do not weigh our merits, but pardon
    our offences,
and fill us all who share in this
    holy communion
with your grace and heavenly blessing.

Through Jesus Christ our Lord,
by whom, and with whom, and in whom,
in the unity of the Holy Spirit,
all honour and glory be yours, almighty Father,
now and for ever. **Amen.**

Silence may be kept.

THE COMMUNION

THE BREAKING OF THE BREAD AND
THE GIVING OF THE BREAD AND CUP

42   THE LORD'S PRAYER is said either as follows or in its traditional form.

President   As our Saviour taught us, so we pray.

All   **Our Father in heaven,**   *or*   Our Father, who art in heaven,
hallowed be your name,   hallowed be thy name;
your kingdom come,   thy kingdom come;
your will be done,   thy will be done;
on earth as in heaven.   on earth as it is in heaven.
Give us today our daily bread.   Give us this day our daily bread.
Forgive us our sins   And forgive us our trespasses,
as we forgive those   as we forgive those
   who sin against us.   who trespass against us.
Lead us not into temptation   And lead us not into temptation;
but deliver us from evil.   but deliver us from evil.

For the kingdom, the power,   For thine is the kingdom,
  and the glory are yours   the power, and the glory,
now and for ever. Amen.   for ever and ever. Amen.

43   The president breaks the consecrated bread, saying

        We break this bread
        to share in the body of Christ.
All   **Though we are many, we are one body,**
        because we all share in one bread.

44   Either here or during the distribution one of the following anthems may be said.

        Lamb of God, you take away the sins of
          the world:
        have mercy on us.

        Lamb of God, you take away the sins of
          the world:
        have mercy on us.

Lamb of God, you take away the sins of
the world:
grant us peace.

or Jesus, Lamb of God: have mercy on us.
Jesus, bearer of our sins: have mercy on us.
Jesus, redeemer of the world: give us
your peace.

45 Before the distribution the president says

Draw near with faith. Receive the body of our
Lord Jesus Christ which he gave for you, and his
blood which he shed for you.

Eat and drink in remembrance that he died for
you, and feed on him in your hearts by faith with
thanksgiving.

Additional words of invitation may be used (see section 85).

46 The president and people receive the communion. At the
distribution the minister says to each communicant

The body of Christ keep you in eternal life.
The blood of Christ keep you in eternal life.

or The body of Christ.
The blood of Christ.

The communicant replies each time **Amen**, and then
receives.

Alternative words of distribution may be found in section 66.

47 During the distribution HYMNS and ANTHEMS may be
sung.

48 If either or both of the consecrated elements be likely to prove insufficient, the president himself returns to the holy table and adds more, saying these words.

> Father, giving thanks over the bread and the cup according to the institution of your Son Jesus Christ, who said, Take, eat; this is my body (*and/or* Drink this; this is my blood), we pray that this bread/wine also may be to us his body/blood, to be received in remembrance of him.

49 Any consecrated bread and wine which is not required for purposes of communion is consumed at the end of the distribution or after the service.

AFTER COMMUNION

50 AN APPROPRIATE SENTENCE may be said and A HYMN may be sung.

51 Either or both of the following prayers or other suitable prayers are said (see section 86).

52 President   Father of all, we give you thanks and praise, that when we were still far off you met us in your Son and brought us home. Dying and living, he declared your love, gave us grace, and opened the gate of glory. May we who share Christ's body live his risen life; we who drink his cup bring life to others; we whom the Spirit lights give light to the world. Keep us firm in the hope you have set before us, so we and all your children shall be free, and the whole earth live to praise your name; through Christ our Lord. **Amen.**

or

53 **All**   **Almighty God,**
we thank you for feeding us
with the body and blood of your Son
    Jesus Christ.
Through him we offer you our souls and bodies
to be a living sacrifice.
Send us out
in the power of your Spirit
to live and work
to your praise and glory. Amen.

THE DISMISSAL

54 The president may say this or an alternative BLESSING
(section 77).

The peace of God, which passes all
understanding, keep your hearts and minds in
the knowledge and love of God, and of his Son
Jesus Christ our Lord; and the blessing of God
almighty, the Father, the Son, and the Holy
Spirit, be among you, and remain with you
always. **Amen.**

55 President Go in peace to love and serve the Lord.
    All   **In the name of Christ. Amen.**

or

President Go in the peace of Christ.
    All   **Thanks be to God.**

From Easter Day to Pentecost 'Alleluia! Alleluia!' may be
added after both the versicle and the response.

56 The ministers and people depart.

The Order following the pattern of the Book of Common Prayer
(continued from section 22)

57 The priest prepares the bread and wine on the holy table, the offerings of the people may be presented, and A HYMN may be sung.

58 THE COMMANDMENTS (section 78) or the following SUMMARY OF THE LAW may be said.

Minister   Our Lord Jesus Christ said: The first commandment is this: 'Hear, O Israel, the Lord our God is the only Lord. You shall love the Lord your God with all your heart, with all your soul, with all your mind, and with all your strength.' The second is this: 'Love your neighbour as yourself.' There is no other commandment greater than these.

All   **Amen. Lord, have mercy.**

59 The priest invites the congregation to confess their sins in these or other suitable words (see section 25). Alternative confessions may be used (see section 80).

Let us confess our sins, in penitence and faith, firmly resolved to keep God's commandments and to live in love and peace with all men.

60 All   **Almighty God, our heavenly Father, we have sinned against you and against our fellow men, in thought and word and deed, through negligence, through weakness, through our own deliberate fault. We are truly sorry, and repent of all our sins. For the sake of your Son Jesus Christ, who died for us,**

> forgive us all that is past;
> and grant that we may serve you in newness
>   of life
> to the glory of your name. **Amen.**

61 Priest Almighty God,
who forgives all who truly repent,
have mercy upon *you*,
pardon and deliver *you* from all *your* sins,
confirm and strengthen *you* in all goodness,
and keep *you* in life eternal;
through Jesus Christ our Lord. **Amen.**

62 The priest says these SENTENCES.

> Hear the words of comfort our Saviour Christ
> says to all who truly turn to him:
> Come to me, all who labour and are heavy
> laden, and I will give you rest. *Matthew 11.28*

> God so loved the world that he gave his only
> Son, that whoever believes in him should not
> perish but have eternal life. *John 3.16*

> Hear what Saint Paul says:
> This saying is true and worthy of full
> acceptance, that Christ Jesus came into the
> world to save sinners. *1 Timothy 1.15*

> Hear what Saint John says:
> If anyone sins, we have an advocate with the
> Father, Jesus Christ the righteous; and he
> is the propitiation for our sins. *1 John 2.1*

63 Priest Lift up your hearts.
    All   **We lift them to the Lord.**

    Priest Let us give thanks to the Lord our God.
    All   **It is right to give him thanks and praise.**

| Priest | It is indeed right,
it is our duty and our joy,
at all times and in all places
to give you thanks and praise,
holy Father, heavenly King,
almighty and eternal God,
through Jesus Christ our Lord. |

PROPER PREFACE, when appropriate (section 76)

Therefore with angels and archangels,
and with all the company of heaven,
we proclaim your great and glorious name,
for ever praising you and saying:

| All | Holy, holy, holy Lord,
God of power and might,
heaven and earth are full of your glory.
Hosanna in the highest. |

64 All
We do not presume
to come to this your table, merciful Lord,
trusting in our own righteousness,
but in your manifold and great mercies.
We are not worthy
so much as to gather up the crumbs under
your table.
But you are the same Lord
whose nature is always to have mercy.
Grant us therefore, gracious Lord,
so to eat the flesh of your dear Son
Jesus Christ
and to drink his blood,
that we may evermore dwell in him
and he in us. Amen.

65 Priest
Almighty God, our heavenly Father,
in your tender mercy
you gave your only Son Jesus Christ
to suffer death upon the cross for
our redemption;
he made there

a full atonement for the sins of the
    whole world,
offering once for all his one sacrifice
    of himself;
he instituted,
and in his holy gospel commanded us
    to continue,
a perpetual memory of his precious death
until he comes again.

Hear us, merciful Father,
we humbly pray,
and grant that we who receive these gifts of
    your creation,
this bread and this wine,
according to your Son our Saviour Jesus
    Christ's holy institution,
in remembrance of the death that he suffered,
may be partakers of his most blessed body
    and blood;

Who in the same night that he was betrayed,
Here the priest takes the paten.

took bread and gave you thanks;
he broke it, *Here he breaks the bread.*
and gave it to his disciples, saying,
Take, eat;
Here he lays his hand on all the bread.

this is my body which is given for you;
do this in remembrance of me.
In the same way, after supper
Here he takes the cup:

he took the cup and gave you thanks;
he gave it to them, saying,
Drink this, all of you;
*Here he lays his hand on all the vessels of wine to be
consecrated.*

this is my blood of the new covenant,
which is shed for you and for many for the
    forgiveness of sins.
Do this, as often as you drink it,
in remembrance of me. **Amen.**

66 The priest and people receive the communion. At the distribution the minister says to the communicants the following words, or those in sections 45 and 46.

> The body of our Lord Jesus Christ, which was given for you, preserve your body and soul to eternal life. Take and eat this in remembrance that Christ died for you, and feed on him in your heart by faith with thanksgiving.

> The blood of our Lord Jesus Christ, which was shed for you, preserve your body and soul to eternal life. Drink this in remembrance that Christ's blood was shed for you, and be thankful.

67 If either or both of the consecrated elements be likely to prove insufficient, the priest himself returns to the holy table and adds more, and consecrates according to the form in section 65, beginning, 'Our Saviour Christ in the same night . . .', for the bread, and at 'In the same way, after supper our Saviour . . .', for the cup.

68 Any consecrated bread and wine which is not required for purposes of communion is consumed at the end of the distribution or after the service.

69 THE LORD'S PRAYER is said either as follows or in its traditional form.

Priest   As our Saviour taught us, so we pray.

All Our Father in heaven,
hallowed be your name,
your kingdom come,
your will be done,
on earth as in heaven.
Give us today our daily bread.
Forgive us our sins
as we forgive those
    who sin against us.

or Our Father, who art in heaven,
hallowed be thy name;
thy kingdom come;
thy will be done;
on earth as it is in heaven.
Give us this day our daily bread.
And forgive us our trespasses,
as we forgive those
    who trespass against us.

Lead us not into temptation but deliver us from evil.	And lead us not into temptation; but deliver us from evil.
For the kingdom, the power, and the glory are yours now and for ever. Amen.	For thine is the kingdom, the power, and the glory, for ever and ever. Amen.

70   One or other of the following prayers or one of those at sections 52 and 53 is used.

71

Lord and heavenly Father, we your servants entirely desire your fatherly goodness mercifully to accept this our sacrifice of praise and thanksgiving, and to grant that, by the merits and death of your Son Jesus Christ, and through faith in his blood, we and your whole Church may receive forgiveness of our sins and all other benefits of his passion.

And here we offer and present to you, O Lord, ourselves, our souls and bodies, to be a reasonable, holy, and living sacrifice, humbly beseeching you that all we who are partakers of this holy communion may be fulfilled with your grace and heavenly benediction.

And although we are unworthy, through our many sins, to offer you any sacrifice, yet we pray that you will accept this, the duty and service that we owe, not weighing our merits but pardoning our offences, through Jesus Christ our Lord; by whom and with whom, in the unity of the Holy Spirit, all honour and glory are yours, Father almighty, now and for ever. **Amen.**

or

72

Almighty and everliving God, we heartily thank you that you graciously feed us, who have duly received these holy mysteries, with the spiritual food of the most precious body and blood of

your Son our Saviour Jesus Christ, and assure
us thereby of your favour and goodness towards
us and that we are true members of the mystical
body of your Son, the blessed company of all
faithful people, and are also heirs, through
hope, of your eternal kingdom, by the merits of
the most precious death and passion of your
dear Son. And we humbly beseech you,
heavenly Father, so to assist us with your grace,
that we may continue in that holy fellowship,
and do all such good works as you have
prepared for us to walk in; through Jesus Christ
our Lord, to whom, with you and the Holy
Spirit, be all honour and glory, now and for
ever. **Amen.**

73   GLORIA IN EXCELSIS or A HYMN may be sung.

All   **Glory to God in the highest,
and peace to his people on earth.**

**Lord God, heavenly King,
almighty God and Father,
we worship you, we give you thanks,
we praise you for your glory.**

**Lord Jesus Christ, only Son of the Father,
Lord God, Lamb of God,
you take away the sin of the world:
have mercy on us;
you are seated at the right hand of the Father:
receive our prayer.**

**For you alone are the Holy One,
you alone are the Lord,
you alone are the Most High,
Jesus Christ,
with the Holy Spirit,
in the glory of God the Father. Amen.**

74   Priest   The peace of God, which passes all understanding, keep your hearts and minds in the knowledge and love of God, and of his Son Jesus Christ our Lord; and the blessing of God almighty, the Father, the Son, and the Holy Spirit, be among you, and remain with you always. **Amen.**

75   The ministers and people depart.

Appendices

PROPER PREFACES

Suitable for use with all Eucharistic Prayers (sections 38, 39, 40, and 41) and the Order following the pattern of the Book of Common Prayer (section 63), except that Preface (3) is not suitable for use with the Third Eucharistic Prayer.

Advent
1 And now we give you thanks because in his coming as man the day of our deliverance has dawned; and through him you will make all things new, as he comes in power and triumph to judge the world.

2 And now we give you thanks because you prepared the way of your Son Jesus Christ by the preaching of your servant John the Baptist, who proclaimed him as the Lamb of God, our Saviour.

The Incarnation
3 And now we give you thanks because by the power of the Holy Spirit he took our nature upon him and was born of the Virgin Mary his mother, that being himself without sin he might make us clean from all sin.

4 And now we give you thanks because in the incarnation of the Word a new light has dawned upon the world; you have become one with us that we might become one with you in your glorious kingdom.

5 And now we give you thanks because in coming to dwell among us as man, he revealed the radiance of your glory, and brought us out of darkness into your own marvellous light.

6 And now we give you thanks because in choosing the blessed Virgin Mary to be the mother of your Son you have exalted the humble and meek. Your angel hailed her as most highly favoured; with all generations we call her blessed, and with her we rejoice and magnify your holy name.

7 And now we give you thanks because in his earthly childhood you entrusted him to the care of a human family. In Mary and Joseph you give us an example of love and devotion to him, and also a pattern of family life.

Lent
8 And now we give you thanks because through him you have given us the spirit of discipline, that we may triumph over evil and grow in grace.

The Cross
9 And now we give you thanks because for our sins he was lifted high upon the cross that he might draw the whole world to himself; and, by his suffering and death, became the source of eternal salvation for all who put their trust in him.

10 And now we give you thanks because for our salvation he was obedient even to death on the cross. The tree of shame was made the tree of glory; and where life was lost, there life has been restored.

Maundy Thursday
11 And now we give you thanks because when his hour had come, in his great love he gave this supper to his disciples, that we might proclaim his death, and feast with him in his kingdom.

The Blessing of the Oils
12 And now we give you thanks because by your Holy Spirit you anointed your only Son to be servant of all and ordained that he should enter into his kingdom through suffering. In your wisdom and love you call your Church to serve the world, to share in Christ's suffering and to reveal his glory.

The Resurrection
13 And now we give you thanks because you raised him gloriously from the dead. For he is the true Paschal Lamb who was offered for us and has taken away the sin of the world. By his death he has destroyed death, and by his rising again he has restored to us eternal life.

14 And now we give you thanks because in his victory over the grave a new age has dawned, the long reign of sin is ended, a broken world is being renewed, and man is once again made whole.

15 And now we give you thanks because through him you have given us eternal life, and delivered us from the bondage of sin and the fear of death into the glorious liberty of the children of God.

16 And now we give you thanks because through him you have given us the hope of a glorious resurrection; so that, although death comes to us all, yet we rejoice in the promise of eternal life; for to your faithful people life is changed, not taken away; and when our mortal flesh is laid aside, an everlasting dwelling place is made ready for us in heaven.

The Ascension
17 And now we give you thanks because you have highly exalted him, and given him the name which is above all other names, that at the name of Jesus every knee shall bow.

Pentecost: Baptism and Confirmation
18 And now we give you thanks because by the Holy Spirit you lead us into all truth, and give us power to proclaim your gospel to the nations, and to serve you as a royal priesthood.

Trinity Sunday
19 And now we give you thanks because you have revealed your glory as the glory of your Son and of the Holy Spirit: three persons equal in majesty, undivided in splendour, yet one Lord, one God, ever to be worshipped and adored.

The Transfiguration
20 And now we give you thanks because the divine glory of the incarnate Word shone forth upon the holy mountain; and your own voice from heaven proclaimed your beloved Son.

St Michael and All Angels
21 Through him the archangels sing your praise, the angels
fulfil your commands, the cherubim and seraphim
continually proclaim your holiness; the whole company of
heaven glorifies your name and rejoices to do your will.
Therefore we pray that our voices may be heard with theirs,
for ever praising you and saying:

All   **Holy, holy, holy Lord . . .**

All Saints' Day
22 And now we give you thanks for the hope to which you
call us in your Son, that following in the faith of all your
saints, we may run with perseverance the race that is set
before us, and with them receive the unfading crown of
glory.

Apostles and Evangelists
23 And now we give you thanks because your Son Jesus
Christ after his resurrection sent forth his apostles and
evangelists to preach the gospel to all nations and to teach us
the way of truth.

Martyrs
24 And now we give you thanks that in the witness of your
martyrs who followed Christ even to death you revealed
your power made perfect in our human weakness.

Saints' Days
25 And now we give you thanks for the work of your grace
in the life of Saint N and that by the same grace you lead us in
the way of holiness setting before us the vision of your glory.

Dedication
26 And now we give you thanks for your blessing on this
house of prayer, where through your grace we offer you the
sacrifice of praise, and are built by your Spirit into a temple
made without hands, even the body of your Son
Jesus Christ.

Marriage

27 And now we give you thanks because you have made the union between Christ and his Church a pattern for the marriage between husband and wife.

Ordination

28 And now we give you thanks because within the royal priesthood of your Church you ordain ministers to proclaim the word of God, to care for your people and to celebrate the sacraments of the new covenant.

Unity

29 And now we give you thanks because of the unity that you have given us in your Son and that you are the God and Father of us all, above all and through all and in all.

Baptism

30 And now we give you thanks because through baptism we have been buried with Christ so that we may rise with him to the new life.

Suitable for use with the Fourth Eucharistic Prayer (section 41) and the Order following the pattern of the Book of Common Prayer (section 63).

Sundays

31 And now we give you thanks because you are the source of light and life; you made us in your image, and called us to new life in him.

32 And now we give you thanks because on the first day of the week he overcame death and the grave and opened to us the way of everlasting life.

33 And now we give you thanks because by water and the Holy Spirit you have made us in him a new people to show forth your glory.

Advent
Christ the Sun of Righteousness shine upon you and scatter
the darkness from before your path; and the blessing . . .

Christmas
Christ, who by his incarnation gathered into one all things
earthly and heavenly, fill you with his joy and peace; and the
blessing . . .

or

Christ the Son of God, born of Mary, fill you with his grace to
trust his promises and obey his will; and the blessing . . .

Epiphany
Christ the Son of God gladden your hearts with the good
news of his kingdom; and the blessing . . .

Ash Wednesday to Lent 4
Christ give you grace to grow in holiness, to deny
yourselves, take up your cross, and follow him; and the
blessing . . .

Lent 5 and Holy Week
Christ crucified draw you to himself, to find in him a sure
ground for faith, a firm support for hope, and the assurance
of sins forgiven; and the blessing . . .

Easter
The God of peace, who brought again from the dead our
Lord Jesus, that great shepherd of the sheep, through
the blood of the eternal covenant, make you perfect in every
good work to do his will, working in you that which is
well-pleasing in his sight; and the blessing . . .

or

The God of peace, who brought again from the dead our Lord Jesus, that great shepherd of the sheep, make you perfect in every good work to do his will; and the blessing . . .

or

God the Father, by whose glory Christ was raised from the dead, strengthen you to walk with him in his risen life; and the blessing . . .

or

God, who through the resurrection of our Lord Jesus Christ has given us the victory, give you joy and peace in your faith; and the blessing . . .

Ascension
Christ our king make you faithful and strong to do his will, that you may reign with him in glory; and the blessing . . .

Pentecost
The Spirit of truth lead you into all truth, give you grace to confess that Jesus Christ is Lord, and to proclaim the word and works of God; and the blessing . . .

Trinity Sunday
God the Holy Trinity make you strong in faith and love, defend you on every side, and guide you in truth and peace; and the blessing . . .

Saints' Days
God give you grace to follow his saints in faith and hope and love; and the blessing . . .

or

God give you grace to follow his saints in faith and truth and gentleness; and the blessing . . .

or

God give you grace to share the inheritance of his saints in glory; and the blessing . . .

Unity

Christ the Good Shepherd, who laid down his life for the sheep, draw you and all who hear his voice to be one within one fold; and the blessing . . .

General

The God of all grace who called you to his eternal glory in Christ Jesus, establish, strengthen and settle you in the faith; and the blessing . . .

or

God, who from the death of sin raised you to new life in Christ, keep you from falling and set you in the presence of his glory; and the blessing . . .

or

Christ who has nourished us with himself the living bread, make you one in praise and love, and raise you up at the last day; and the blessing . . .

or

The God of peace fill you with all joy and hope in believing; and the blessing . . .

78 **THE COMMANDMENTS**

Either A:

Minister   Our Lord Jesus Christ said, If you love me, keep my commandments; happy are those who hear the word of God and keep it. Hear then these commandments which God has given to his people, and take them to heart.

                I am the Lord your God: you shall have no other gods but me.
                You shall love the Lord your God with all your heart, with all your soul, with all your mind, and with all your strength.

All   **Amen. Lord, have mercy.**

Minister	You shall not make for yourself any idol. God is spirit, and those who worship him must worship in spirit and in truth.
All	**Amen. Lord, have mercy.**

Minister	You shall not dishonour the name of the Lord your God. You shall worship him with awe and reverence.
All	**Amen. Lord, have mercy.**

Minister	Remember the Lord's day and keep it holy. Christ is risen from the dead: set your minds on things that are above, not on things that are on the earth.
All	**Amen. Lord, have mercy.**

Minister	Honour your father and mother. Live as servants of God; honour all men; love the brotherhood.
All	**Amen. Lord, have mercy.**

Minister	You shall not commit murder. Be reconciled to your brother; overcome evil with good.
All	**Amen. Lord, have mercy.**

Minister	You shall not commit adultery. Know that your body is a temple of the Holy Spirit.
All	**Amen. Lord, have mercy.**

Minister	You shall not steal. Be honest in all that you do and care for those in need.
All	**Amen. Lord, have mercy.**

Minister	You shall not be a false witness. Let everyone speak the truth.
All	**Amen. Lord, have mercy.**

| Minister | You shall not covet anything which belongs to your neighbour. Remember the words of the Lord Jesus: It is more blessed to give than to receive. Love your neighbour as yourself, for love is the fulfilling of the law. |
| All | **Amen. Lord, have mercy.** |

or B:

| Minister | God spoke all these words, saying, I am the Lord your God (who brought you out of the land of Egypt, out of the house of bondage). You shall have no other gods before me. |
| All | **Amen. Lord, have mercy.** |

| Minister | You shall not make for yourself a graven image (or any likeness of anything that is in heaven above, or that is in the earth beneath, or that is in the water under the earth; you shall not bow down to them or serve them; for I the Lord your God am a jealous God, visiting the iniquity of the fathers upon the children to the third and the fourth generation of those who hate me, but showing steadfast love to thousands of those who love me and keep my commandments). |
| All | **Amen. Lord, have mercy.** |

| Minister | You shall not take the name of the Lord your God in vain (for the Lord will not hold him guiltless who takes his name in vain). |
| All | **Amen. Lord, have mercy.** |

| Minister | Remember the sabbath day, to keep it holy. (Six days you shall labour, and do all your work; but the seventh day is a sabbath to the Lord your God; in it you shall not do any work, you, or your son, or your daughter, your manservant, or your maidservant, or your cattle, or the sojourner who is within your gates; for in |

six days the Lord made heaven and earth, the sea, and all that is in them, and rested the seventh day; therefore the Lord blessed the sabbath day and hallowed it.)

All   **Amen. Lord, have mercy.**

Minister   Honour your father and your mother (that your days may be long in the land which the Lord your God gives you).

All   **Amen. Lord, have mercy.**

Minister   You shall not kill.
All   **Amen. Lord, have mercy.**

Minister   You shall not commit adultery.
All   **Amen. Lord, have mercy.**

Minister   You shall not steal.
All   **Amen. Lord, have mercy.**

Minister   You shall not bear false witness against your neighbour.
All   **Amen. Lord, have mercy.**

Minister   You shall not covet (your neighbour's house; you shall not covet your neighbour's wife, or his manservant, or his maidservant, or his ox, or his ass, or) anything that is your neighbour's.
All   **Lord, have mercy on us, and write all these your laws in our hearts.**

79   KYRIE ELEISON

Section 9 may be said in one of the following forms.

Lord, have mercy (upon us.)   Kyrie eleison.
Lord, have mercy (upon us.)   **Kyrie eleison.**
Lord, have mercy (upon us.)   Kyrie eleison.

Christ, have mercy (upon us.)	**Christe eleison.**
Christ, have mercy (upon us.)	Christe eleison.
Christ, have mercy (upon us.)	**Christe eleison.**
Lord, have mercy (upon us.)	Kyrie eleison.
Lord, have mercy (upon us.)	**Kyrie eleison.**
Lord, have mercy (upon us.)	Kyrie eleison.

80 ALTERNATIVE CONFESSIONS

Either A:

All   Almighty God, our heavenly Father,
we have sinned against you and against our
    fellow men,
in thought and word and deed,
in the evil we have done
and in the good we have not done,
through ignorance, through weakness,
through our own deliberate fault.
We are truly sorry,
and repent of all our sins.
For the sake of your Son Jesus Christ, who
    died for us,
forgive us all that is past;
and grant that we may serve you in newness
    of life
to the glory of your name. Amen.

or B:

All   Almighty God, our heavenly Father,
we have sinned against you,
through our own fault,
in thought and word and deed,
and in what we have left undone.
For your Son our Lord Jesus Christ's sake,
forgive us all that is past;
and grant that we may serve you in newness
    of life
to the glory of your name. Amen.

or C:

All
Father eternal, giver of light and grace,
we have sinned against you and against our
    fellow men,
in what we have thought,
in what we have said and done,
through ignorance, through weakness,
through our own deliberate fault.
We have wounded your love,
and marred your image in us.
We are sorry and ashamed,
and repent of all our sins.
For the sake of your Son Jesus Christ, who
    died for us,
forgive us all that is past;
and lead us out from darkness
to walk as children of light. Amen.

81 ALTERNATIVE FORMS OF INTERCESSION

Either A:

Minister
Let us pray for the whole Church of God in Christ Jesus, and for all men according to their needs.

O God, the creator and preserver of all mankind, we pray for men of every race, and in every kind of need: make your ways known on earth, your saving power among all nations. (Especially we pray for . . .)
Lord, in your mercy

All
hear our prayer.

Minister
We pray for your Church throughout the world: guide and govern us by your Holy Spirit, that all who profess and call themselves Christians

	may be led into the way of truth, and hold the faith in unity of spirit, in the bond of peace, and in righteousness of life. (Especially we pray for . . .) Lord, in your mercy
All	**hear our prayer.**

Minister	We commend to your fatherly goodness all who are anxious or distressed in mind or body; comfort and relieve them in their need; give them patience in their sufferings, and bring good out of their troubles. (Especially we pray for . . .) Merciful Father,
All	**accept these prayers for the sake of your Son, our Saviour Jesus Christ. Amen.**

or B:

Minister	In the power of the Spirit and in union with Christ, let us pray to the Father.
	Hear our prayers, O Lord our God.
All	**Hear us, good Lord.**

Minister	Govern and direct your holy Church; fill it with love and truth; and grant it that unity which is your will.
All	**Hear us, good Lord.**

Minister	Give us boldness to preach the gospel in all the world, and to make disciples of all the nations.
All	**Hear us, good Lord.**

Minister	Enlighten your ministers with knowledge and understanding, that by their teaching and their lives they may proclaim your word.
All	**Hear us, good Lord.**

Minister	Give your people grace to hear and receive your word, and to bring forth the fruit of the Spirit.
All	**Hear us, good Lord.**

Minister	Bring into the way of truth all who have erred and are deceived.
All	**Hear us, good Lord.**

Minister	Strengthen those who stand; comfort and help the faint-hearted; raise up the fallen; and finally beat down Satan under our feet.
All	**Hear us, good Lord.**

Minister	Guide the leaders of the nations into the ways of peace and justice.
All	**Hear us, good Lord.**

Minister	Guard and strengthen your servant Elizabeth our Queen, that she may put her trust in you, and seek your honour and glory.
All	**Hear us, good Lord.**

Minister	Endue the High Court of Parliament and all the Ministers of the Crown with wisdom and understanding.
All	**Hear us, good Lord.**

Minister	Bless those who administer the law, that they may uphold justice, honesty, and truth.
All	**Hear us, good Lord.**

Minister	Teach us to use the fruits of the earth to your glory, and for the good of all mankind.
All	**Hear us, good Lord.**

Minister	Bless and keep all your people.
All	**Hear us, good Lord.**

Minister	Help and comfort the lonely, the bereaved, and the oppressed.
All	**Lord, have mercy.**
Minister	Keep in safety those who travel, and all who are in danger.
All	**Lord, have mercy.**
Minister	Heal the sick in body and mind, and provide for the homeless, the hungry, and the destitute.
All	**Lord, have mercy.**
Minister	Show your pity on prisoners and refugees, and all who are in trouble.
All	**Lord, have mercy.**
Minister	Forgive our enemies, persecutors, and slanderers, and turn their hearts.
All	**Lord, have mercy.**
Minister	Hear us as we remember those who have died in the peace of Christ, both those who have confessed the faith and those whose faith is known to you alone, and grant us with them a share in your eternal kingdom.
All	**Lord, have mercy.**
Minister	Father, you hear those who pray in the name of your Son: grant that what we have asked in faith we may obtain according to your will; through Jesus Christ our Lord. **Amen.**

82 ALTERNATIVE PRAYER OF HUMBLE ACCESS (section 29)

Most merciful Lord,
your love compels us to come in.
Our hands were unclean,
our hearts were unprepared;
we were not fit
even to eat the crumbs from under your table.
But you, Lord, are the God of our salvation,
and share your bread with sinners.
So cleanse and feed us
with the precious body and blood of your Son,
that he may live in us and we in him;
and that we, with the whole company of Christ,
may sit and eat in your kingdom. Amen.

83 A SELECTION OF OTHER INTRODUCTORY WORDS TO THE PEACE (section 30)

Advent, Christmas, Epiphany
Our Saviour Christ is the Prince of Peace; of the increase of
his government and of peace there shall be no end.

Lent
Being justified by faith, we have peace with God through
our Lord Jesus Christ.

Easter, Ascension
The risen Christ came and stood among his disciples and
said, Peace be with you. Then they were glad when they saw
the Lord.

Pentecost
The fruit of the Spirit is love, joy, peace. If we live in the
Spirit, let us walk in the Spirit.

Saints' Days
We are fellow-citizens with the saints, and of the household
of God, through Christ our Lord who came and preached
peace to those who were far off and those who were near.

President	The Lord be with you or The Lord is here.
All	**and also with you.　His Spirit is with us.**

President	Lift up your hearts.
All	**We lift them to the Lord.**

President	Let us give thanks to the Lord our God.
All	**It is right to give him thanks and praise.**

President　It is indeed right,
it is our duty and our joy,
to give you thanks, holy Father,
through Jesus Christ our Lord.

Through him you have created us in your image;
through him you have freed us from sin
and death;
through him you have made us your own people
by the gift of the Holy Spirit.

Hear us, Father,
through Christ your Son our Lord,
and grant that by the power of your
Holy Spirit
these gifts of bread and wine
may be to us his body and his blood;

Who in the same night that he was betrayed,
took bread and gave you thanks;
he broke it and gave it to his disciples,
saying,
Take, eat; this is my body which is given
for you;
do this in remembrance of me.
In the same way, after supper
he took the cup and gave you thanks;
he gave it to them, saying,
Drink this, all of you;
this is my blood of the new covenant,

which is shed for you and for many for the
    forgiveness of sins.
Do this, as often as you drink it,
in remembrance of me.

Therefore, Father,
proclaiming his saving death and resurrection
and looking for his coming in glory,
we celebrate with this bread and this cup
his one perfect sacrifice.

Accept through him, our great high priest,
this our sacrifice of thanks and praise,
and grant that we who eat this bread and
    drink this cup
may be renewed by your Spirit and grow into
    his likeness;

Through Jesus Christ our Lord,
by whom, and with whom, and in whom,
all honour and glory be yours, Father,
now and for ever. **Amen.**

85 ADDITIONAL WORDS OF INVITATION TO COMMUNION
which may be used after section 45

Either A:

President   Jesus is the Lamb of God
           who takes away the sins of the world.
           Happy are those who are called to his supper.
All   **Lord, I am not worthy to receive you,
           but only say the word, and I shall be healed.**

or B:

President   The gifts of God for the people of God.
All   **Jesus Christ is holy,
           Jesus Christ is Lord,
           to the glory of God the Father.**

President: Alleluia! Christ our Passover is sacrificed for us.
All   Alleluia! Let us keep the feast.

86 ALTERNATIVE FINAL PRAYER
Especially suitable for a service without Communion

All   **Almighty God,**
                we offer you our souls and bodies,
                to be a living sacrifice,
                through Jesus Christ our Lord.
                Send us out into the world
                in the power of your Spirit,
                to live and work
                to your praise and glory. Amen.

The Order for Holy Communion

Rite B

NOTES

1 **Seasonal Material** The seasonal sentences (sections 1, 43) and blessings (section 54) are optional. Any other appropriate scriptural sentences may be read at sections 1 and 43 at the discretion of the priest and 'Alleluia' may be added to any sentence from Easter Day until Pentecost (Whit Sunday).

2 **1662 Material** It is permitted to use the 1662 text of the Gloria (sections 5, 48), the Creed (section 14), the Intercession (sections 17, 18), the Confession (section 21), the Absolution (section 22), and the Lord's Prayer (sections 33, 36, 44) instead of the texts printed here.

3 **Gloria in excelsis** (section 5) This canticle is also appropriate at sections 1, 11, and 48.

4 **Collects and Readings** The collects and readings are either those set out in this book or those in the Book of Common Prayer, together with any others approved by the General Synod.

5 **The Sermon** The sermon (section 13) is an integral part of the Ministry of the Word. A sermon should normally be preached at all celebrations on Sundays and other Holy Days.

6 **The Peace** The priest may accompany the words of the Peace (sections 24, 25) with a handclasp or similar action; and both the words and the action may be passed through the congregation.

7 **The Prayers of Intercession and The Thanksgiving** (sections 17, 18, and 30, 31) The use of the first Intercession does not presume the use of the first Thanksgiving. Either Prayer of Intercession may be used with either Thanksgiving.

8 **Proper Prefaces** The Proper Prefaces set out for use in the first Thanksgiving and those for Christmas, Passiontide, Easter and Ascension in the second Thanksgiving are obligatory.

9 **The First Thanksgiving** (section 30) The Prayer of Humble Access may, if desired, be said after the Sanctus; and the Thanksgiving may end after the words, 'Do this, as oft as ye shall drink it, in remembrance of me'; in which case the people then say **Amen.**

10 **The Blessing** (section 49) In addition to the blessings provided here and at section 54 the priest may at his discretion use others.

11 **Notices** Banns of marriage and other notices may be published after section 1, section 12, or section 42, if they are not published at section 15.

12 **Hymns, Canticles, The Peace, The Collection and Presentation of the Offerings of the People, and The Preparation of the Gifts of Bread and Wine** Points are indicated for these, but if occasion requires they may occur elsewhere.

13 **Silence** After sections 8, 10, 12, 13, 20, 43 and after the biddings in sections 17, 18 silence may be kept.

14 **A Service without Communion** When there is no communion the minister reads the service as far as the Absolution (section 22) and then adds the Lord's Prayer (section 36), the General Thanksgiving, and/or other prayers at his discretion, ending with the Grace. When such a service is led by a deacon or lay person, 'us' is said instead of 'you' in the Absolution.

The Order for Holy Communion Rite B

THE WORD AND THE PRAYERS

THE PREPARATION

1 At the entry of the ministers A SENTENCE may be used; and A HYMN, A CANTICLE, or A PSALM may be sung.

2 The minister may say

          The Lord be with you
All   **and with thy spirit.**

3 This prayer may be said.

All   **Almighty God,**
               unto whom all hearts be open,
               all desires known,
               and from whom no secrets are hid:
               cleanse the thoughts of our hearts
               by the inspiration of thy Holy Spirit,
               that we may perfectly love thee,
               and worthily magnify thy holy name;
               through Christ our Lord. Amen.

4 One of the following may be used.

Either THE COMMANDMENTS (section 55);
or THE SUMMARY OF THE LAW (section 56);
or KYRIE ELEISON in English or Greek (section 57),
each petition being said once, twice, or three times.

5   GLORIA IN EXCELSIS may be said.

All   Glory be to God on high,
and in earth peace, good will towards men.

We praise thee, we bless thee,
we worship thee, we glorify thee,
we give thanks to thee for thy great glory,
O Lord God, heavenly King,
God the Father almighty.

O Lord, the only-begotten Son, Jesus Christ:
O Lord God, Lamb of God, Son of the Father,
that takest away the sins of the world,
have mercy upon us.
Thou that takest away the sins of the world,
receive our prayer.
Thou that sittest at the right hand of God
   the Father,
have mercy upon us.

For thou only art holy;
thou only art the Lord;
thou only, O Christ,
with the Holy Ghost,
art the Most High,
in the glory of God the Father. Amen.

6   THE COLLECT

THE MINISTRY OF THE WORD

7   Either two or three readings from scripture follow, the last of
which is always the Gospel.

8   **Sit**
OLD TESTAMENT READING

At the end the reader may say

        This is the word of the Lord.
All   **Thanks be to God.**

9   A PSALM may be used.

10   **Sit**
     NEW TESTAMENT READING (EPISTLE)

     At the end the reader may say

                   This is the word of the Lord.
     All   **Thanks be to God.**

11   A CANTICLE, A HYMN, or A PSALM may be used.

12   **Stand**
     THE GOSPEL. When it is announced

     All   **Glory be to thee, O Lord.**

     At the end the reader says

                   This is the Gospel of Christ.
     All   **Praise be to thee, O Christ.**

13   **Sit**
     THE SERMON

14   **Stand**
     THE NICENE CREED is said on Sundays and other Holy
     Days, and may be said on other days.

     All   **I believe in one God**
                   the Father almighty,
                   maker of heaven and earth,
                   and of all things visible and invisible:

                   And in one Lord Jesus Christ,
                   the only-begotten Son of God,
                   begotten of his Father before all worlds,
                   God of God, Light of Light,
                   very God of very God,
                   begotten, not made,
                   being of one substance with the Father,
                   by whom all things were made;

                              Holy Communion B   181

who for us men and for our salvation
came down from heaven,
and was incarnate by the Holy Ghost
  of the Virgin Mary,
and was made man,
and was crucified also for us
  under Pontius Pilate.
He suffered and was buried,
and the third day he rose again
according to the scriptures,
and ascended into heaven,
and sitteth on the right hand of the Father.
And he shall come again with glory
to judge both the quick and the dead:
whose kingdom shall have no end.

And I believe in the Holy Ghost,
the Lord, the Giver of life,
who proceedeth from the Father
  and the Son,
who with the Father and the Son together
  is worshipped and glorified,
who spake by the prophets.
And I believe one holy catholic and
  apostolic Church.
I acknowledge one baptism for the
  remission of sins.
And I look for the resurrection
  of the dead,
and the life of the world to come. Amen.

PRAYERS OF INTERCESSION

15   Banns of marriage and other notices may be published;
the offerings of the people may be collected and presented;
a hymn may be sung; and verses of scripture may be read.

16   INTERCESSIONS are led by the priest, or by others. These
may be introduced by biddings.

It is not necessary to include specific subjects in any section
of the following prayers.

The set passages may follow one another as a continuous whole, or this versicle and response may be used after each paragraph.

Minister   Lord, in thy mercy
All   **hear our prayer.**

Either section 17 or section 18 is used.

17   FIRST INTERCESSION

Minister   Let us pray for the whole Church of God
           in Christ Jesus,
and for all men according to their needs.

Almighty and everliving God, who by thy holy apostle hast taught us to make prayers and supplications, and to give thanks, for all men: we humbly beseech thee most mercifully *(to accept our alms and oblations, and) to receive these our prayers, which we offer unto thy divine majesty; beseeching thee to inspire continually the universal Church with the spirit of truth, unity, and concord; and grant that all they that do confess thy holy name may agree in the truth of thy holy word, and live in unity and godly love.

We beseech thee also to lead all nations in the way of righteousness and peace; and so to direct all kings and rulers, that under them thy people may be godly and quietly governed. And grant unto thy servant Elizabeth our Queen and to all that are put in authority under her, that they may truly and impartially administer justice, to the punishment of wickedness and vice, and to the maintenance of thy true religion and virtue. Give grace, O heavenly Father, to all bishops, priests, and deacons, especially to thy servant N our bishop, that they may both by their life and

*If the offerings of the people have not been presented these words in brackets are omitted.

doctrine set forth thy true and lively word and rightly and duly administer thy holy sacraments.

Guide and prosper, we pray thee, those who are labouring for the spread of thy gospel among the nations, and enlighten with thy Spirit all places of education and learning; that the whole world may be filled with the knowledge of thy truth.

And to all thy people give thy heavenly grace; and specially to this congregation here present, that with meek heart and due reverence, they may hear and receive thy holy word; truly serving thee in holiness and righteousness all the days of their life.

And we most humbly beseech thee of thy goodness, O Lord, to comfort and succour all them who in this transitory life are in trouble, sorrow, need, sickness, or any other adversity.

And we commend to thy gracious keeping, O Lord, all thy servants departed this life in thy faith and fear, beseeching thee, according to thy promises, to grant them refreshment, light, and peace.

And here we give thee most high praise and hearty thanks for all thy saints, who have been the chosen vessels of thy grace, and lights of the world in their several generations; and we pray that, rejoicing in their fellowship and following their good examples, we may be partakers with them of thy heavenly kingdom.

Grant this, O Father, for Jesus Christ's sake, our only mediator and advocate, who liveth and reigneth with thee in the unity of the Holy Spirit, one God, world without end. **Amen.**

The service continues at either section 19 or section 20.

Minister   Let us pray for the whole Church of God
                  in Christ Jesus,
             and for all men according to their needs.

             Almighty God, who hast promised to hear the
             prayers of those who ask in faith:

             Here he may pray for the Church throughout
             the world, especially for the diocese and its
             bishop; and for any particular needs of the
             Church.

             Grant that we and all who confess thy name may
             be united in thy truth, live together in thy love,
             and show forth thy glory in the world.

             Here he may pray for the nations of the world,
             for this kingdom, and for all men in their various
             callings.

             Give wisdom to all in authority, bless Elizabeth
             our Queen, and direct this nation and all nations
             in the ways of justice and of peace; that men may
             honour one another, and seek the common
             good.

             Here he may pray for the local community; for
             families, friends, and particular persons.

             Give grace to us, our families and friends, and to
             all our neighbours in Christ, that we may serve
             him in one another, and love as he loves us.

             Here he may pray for the sick, the poor, and
             those in trouble, and for the needs of particular
             persons.

             Save and comfort those who suffer, that they
             may hold to thee through good and ill, and trust
             in thy unfailing love.

Here he may commemorate the departed; he may commend them by name.

Hear us as we remember those who have died in faith, and grant us with them a share in thy eternal kingdom.

Merciful Father,
All **accept these prayers,**
for the sake of thy Son,
our Saviour Jesus Christ. Amen.

PRAYERS OF PENITENCE

19 The minister may say one or more of
THE COMFORTABLE WORDS.

Hear what comfortable words our Saviour Christ says to all who truly turn to him:
Come unto me, all that travail, and are heavy laden, and I will refresh you.   *Matthew 11.28*

So God loved the world, that he gave his only-begotten Son, to the end that all that believe in him should not perish, but have everlasting life.   *John 3.16*

Hear what Saint Paul says:
This is a true saying and worthy of all men to be received, that Christ Jesus came into the world to save sinners.   *1 Timothy 1.15*

Hear what Saint John says:
If any man sin, we have an advocate with the Father, Jesus Christ the righteous; and he is the propitiation for our sins.   *1 John 2.1*

20	Minister	*(Ye that do truly and earnestly repent you of your sins, and are in love and charity with your neighbours, and intend to lead a new life, following the commandments of God, and walking from henceforth in his holy ways;) draw near with faith, and take this holy sacrament to your comfort; and make your humble confession to almighty God (meekly kneeling upon your knees).
	or	Seeing we have a great high priest who has passed into the heavens, Jesus the Son of God, let us draw near with a true heart, in full assurance of faith, and make our confession to our heavenly Father.
21	**Kneel** **All**	**Almighty God, our heavenly Father,** **we have sinned against thee,** **through our own fault,** **in thought, and word, and deed,** **and in what we have left undone.** **We are heartily sorry** **and repent of all our sins.** **For thy Son our Lord Jesus Christ's sake,** **forgive us all that is past;** **and grant that we may serve thee in newness** **of life,** **to the glory of thy name. Amen.**
22	Priest	Almighty God, who forgives all who truly repent, have mercy upon *you*, pardon and deliver *you* from all *your* sins, confirm and strengthen *you* in all goodness, and keep *you* in life eternal; through Jesus Christ our Lord. **Amen.**

* The words in brackets may be omitted.

We do not presume
to come to this thy table, O merciful Lord,
trusting in our own righteousness,
but in thy manifold and great mercies.
We are not worthy
so much as to gather up the crumbs under
    thy table.
But thou art the same Lord
whose nature is always to have mercy.
Grant us therefore, gracious Lord,
so to eat the flesh of thy dear Son
    Jesus Christ
and to drink his blood,
* (that our sinful bodies may be made clean
    by his body
and our souls washed through his most
    precious blood, and)
that we may evermore dwell in him
and he in us. Amen.

* The words in brackets may be omitted.

THE MINISTRY OF THE SACRAMENT

THE PEACE

24 **Stand**
Priest   We are the Body of Christ.
By one Spirit we were all baptized into
    one body.
Endeavour to keep the unity of the Spirit
in the bond of peace.

He then says

         The peace of the Lord be always with you
All   **and with thy spirit.**

25 All may exchange a sign of peace.

THE PREPARATION OF THE BREAD AND WINE

26 The priest begins THE OFFERTORY.

The bread and the wine are placed on the holy table.

27 The offerings of the people may be collected and presented if
this has not already been done.
These words may be used.

        Thine, O Lord, is the greatness and
          the power
        and the glory and the victory and
          the majesty.
        All that is in heaven and earth is thine.
        All things come of thee, O Lord,
        and of thine own do we give thee.

28 At the preparation of the gifts A HYMN may be sung.

THE THANKSGIVING

29   The priest says THE PRAYER OF CONSECRATION using
      either section 30 or section 31.

30   FIRST THANKSGIVING

Priest	The Lord be with you
All	**and with thy spirit.**

Priest	Lift up your hearts.
All	**We lift them up unto the Lord.**

Priest	Let us give thanks unto the Lord our God.
All	**It is meet and right so to do.**

Priest   It is very meet, right, and our bounden duty,
          that we should at all times and in all places
              give thanks unto thee,
          O Lord, holy Father,
          almighty, everlasting God,
          Creator of heaven and earth,

PROPER PREFACE, when appropriate (section 52)

The following is used when no Proper Preface is provided.

through Jesus Christ our Lord; for he is the true
High Priest, who has washed us from our sins,
and has made us to be a kingdom and priests
unto thee, our God and Father.

Therefore with angels and archangels,
and with all the company of heaven,
we laud and magnify thy glorious name,
evermore praising thee and saying:

**Holy, holy, holy, Lord God of Hosts,
heaven and earth are full of thy glory.
Glory be to thee, O Lord most high. (Amen.)**

**(Blessed is he that cometh in the name of
    the Lord.
Hosanna in the highest.)**

All glory be to thee,
almighty God, our heavenly Father,
who of thy tender mercy
didst give thine only Son Jesus Christ
to suffer death upon the cross
    for our redemption;
who made there,
by his one oblation of himself once offered,
a full, perfect, and sufficient sacrifice,
    oblation, and satisfaction
for the sins of the whole world;
and did institute,
and in his holy gospel command us to continue,
a perpetual memory of that his precious death,
until his coming again.

Hear us, O merciful Father,
we most humbly beseech thee;
and grant that by the power of thy Holy Spirit,
we receiving these thy creatures
    of bread and wine,
according to thy Son our Saviour
    Jesus Christ's holy institution,
in remembrance of his death and passion,
may be partakers
    of his most blessed body and blood.
Who, in the same night that he was betrayed,
took bread;
Here the priest is to take the paten into his hands.

and when he had given thanks,
he brake it, *Here he may break the bread.*
and gave it to his disciples, saying, Take, eat;
Here he is to lay his hand upon the bread.

this is my body which is given for you:
do this in remembrance of me.
Likewise after supper he took the cup;
Here he is to take the cup into his hand.

and when he had given thanks,
he gave it to them, saying, Drink ye all of this;
Here to lay his hand upon the cup.

for this is my blood of the New Testament,
which is shed for you and for many

for the remission of sins:
do this, as oft as ye shall drink it,
in remembrance of me.

Wherefore, O Lord and heavenly Father,
we thy humble servants,
having in remembrance
the precious death and passion of thy dear Son,
his mighty resurrection and glorious ascension,
entirely desire thy fatherly goodness
mercifully to accept this our sacrifice
   of praise and thanksgiving;
most humbly beseeching thee to grant that
by the merits and death of thy Son Jesus Christ,
and through faith in his blood,
we and all thy whole Church
may obtain remission of our sins,
and all other benefits of his passion.
And although we be unworthy
   through our manifold sins
to offer unto thee any sacrifice,
yet we beseech thee to accept
   this our bounden duty and service,
not weighing our merits
   but pardoning our offences.
We pray that all we who are partakers
   of this holy communion
may be fulfilled with thy grace
   and heavenly benediction.
Through Jesus Christ our Lord,
by whom, and with whom, and in whom,
in the unity of the Holy Spirit,
all honour and glory be unto thee,
O Father almighty,
world without end. **Amen.**

Silence may be kept.

The service continues at either section 32 or section 33 or
section 34.

Priest	The Lord be with you
All	**and with thy spirit.**

Priest	Lift up your hearts.
All	**We lift them up unto the Lord.**

Priest	Let us give thanks unto the Lord our God.
All	**It is meet and right so to do.**

Priest   It is very meet, right, and our bounden duty,
that we should at all times and in all places
give thanks unto thee,
O Lord, holy Father,
almighty, everlasting God,
through Jesus Christ
thine only Son our Lord.

Because through him thou hast created
all things from the beginning,
and fashioned us men in thine own image;

through him thou didst redeem us
from the slavery of sin,
giving him to be born as man,
to die upon the cross,
and to rise again for us;

through him thou hast made us a people
for thine own possession,
exalting him to thy right hand on high,
and sending forth through him
thy holy and life-giving Spirit.

PROPER PREFACE, when appropriate (section 53)

Therefore with angels and archangels,
and with all the company of heaven,
we laud and magnify thy glorious name,
evermore praising thee and saying,

**Holy, holy, holy, Lord God of hosts,
heaven and earth are full of thy glory.
Glory be to thee, O Lord most high.**

**(Blessed is he that cometh in the name of
the Lord.
Hosanna in the highest.)**

Hear us, O Father,
through Christ thy Son our Lord;
through him accept our sacrifice of praise;
and grant that by the power of thy Holy Spirit
these gifts of bread and wine
may be unto us his body and blood.

Who, in the same night that he was betrayed,
took bread;
Here the priest is to take the bread into his hands.
and when he had given thanks to thee,
he broke it,
and gave it to his disciples, saying, Take, eat;
this is my body which is given for you:
do this in remembrance of me.

Likewise after supper he took the cup;
Here he is to take the cup into his hands.
and when he had given thanks to thee,
he gave it to them saying, Drink ye all of this;
for this is my blood of the new covenant,
which is shed for you and for many
for the remission of sins:
do this, as oft as ye shall drink it,
in remembrance of me.

Wherefore, O Lord and heavenly Father,
with this bread and this cup
we make the memorial of his saving passion,
his resurrection from the dead,
and his glorious ascension into heaven,
and we look for the coming of his kingdom.
We pray thee to accept this
our duty and service,

and grant that we may so eat and drink
   these holy things
in the presence of thy divine majesty,
that we may be filled with thy grace
   and heavenly blessing.

Through Jesus Christ our Lord,
by whom, and with whom, and in whom,
in the unity of the Holy Spirit,
all honour and glory be unto thee,
O Father almighty,
world without end. **Amen.**

Silence may be kept.

---

32 THE BENEDICTUS may follow, if it has not already
been said.

> **Blessed is he that cometh in the name of
>   the Lord.
> Hosanna in the highest.**

33 The priest and people together say THE LORD'S PRAYER
either here or at section 36, or at section 44. (The text is
printed at section 36.)

THE COMMUNION

THE BREAKING OF THE BREAD AND
THE GIVING OF THE BREAD AND CUP

34 The priest breaks the consecrated bread, if he has not already
done so, saying

> We break this bread
> to share in the body of Christ.

All **Though we are many, we are one body,
because we all share in one bread.**

35 Either here or during the distribution this anthem may be said.

> O Lamb of God,
> that takest away the sins of the world,
> have mercy upon us.
>
> O Lamb of God,
> that takest away the sins of the world,
> have mercy upon us.
>
> O Lamb of God,
> that takest away the sins of the world,
> grant us thy peace.

36 The priest and people may say THE LORD'S PRAYER, if it has not already been said.

Priest　　As our Saviour has taught us, so we pray.
All　　　**Our Father, who art in heaven,**
hallowed be thy name;
thy kingdom come;
thy will be done;
on earth as it is in heaven.
Give us this day our daily bread.
And forgive us our trespasses,
as we forgive those who trespass
against us.
And lead us not into temptation;
but deliver us from evil.

For thine is the kingdom, the power,
and the glory,
for ever and ever. Amen.

37 The priest and people receive the communion.

The communion may be administered in one of the following ways:

The body of our Lord Jesus Christ, which was given for you, preserve your body and soul unto everlasting life. Take and eat this in remembrance that Christ died for you, and feed on him in your heart by faith with thanksgiving.

The blood of our Lord Jesus Christ, which was shed for you, preserve your body and soul unto everlasting life. Drink this in remembrance that Christ's blood was shed for you, and be thankful.

39   or
The priest first says to all the communicants

Draw near and receive the body of our Lord Jesus Christ, which was given for you, and his blood, which was shed for you. Take this in remembrance that Christ died for you, and feed on him in your hearts by faith with thanksgiving.

One of the ministers then delivers the bread to each communicant, saying

The body of Christ.

or   The body of Christ preserve your body and soul unto everlasting life.

or   The body of our Lord Jesus Christ, which was given for you, preserve your body and soul unto everlasting life.

One of the ministers then delivers the cup to each communicant, saying

The blood of Christ.

or   The blood of Christ preserve your body and soul unto everlasting life.

or   The blood of our Lord Jesus Christ, which was shed for you, preserve your body and soul unto everlasting life.

The communicant may reply each time **Amen**, and then receives.

40 During the distribution HYMNS and ANTHEMS may be sung.

41 If either or both of the consecrated elements are likely to prove insufficient, the priest returns to the holy table and adds more, with these words.

> Having given thanks to thee, O Father, over the bread and the cup according to the institution of thy Son Jesus Christ, who said, Take, eat; this is my body (*and/or* Drink this; this is my blood) we pray that this bread/wine also may be to us his body/blood, and be received in remembrance of him.

42 Any consecrated bread and wine which is not required for purposes of communion is consumed at the end of the distribution, or after the service.

AFTER COMMUNION

43 AN APPROPRIATE SENTENCE may be said (pp. 42, 43) and A HYMN may be sung.

44 The priest and people say THE LORD'S PRAYER, if it has not already been said. (The text is printed at section 36.)

45 Either or both of the following PRAYERS or either of those in the Appendices (section 58) are said.

46 Priest   Almighty and everliving God, we most heartily thank thee, for that thou dost vouchsafe to feed us, who have duly received these holy mysteries, with the spiritual food of the most precious body and blood of thy Son our Saviour Jesus Christ; and dost assure us thereby of thy favour and goodness towards us; and that we are very members incorporate in the mystical body of thy Son, which is the blessed company of all faithful people, and are also heirs through hope of thy everlasting kingdom, by the merits of the most precious death and passion of thy dear Son. And we most humbly beseech thee, O heavenly Father, so to assist us with thy grace, that we may continue in that holy fellowship, and do all such good works as thou hast prepared for us to walk in; through Jesus Christ our Lord, to whom, with thee and the Holy Spirit, be all honour and glory, world without end. **Amen.**

47 **All**   **Almighty God,**
we thank thee for feeding us
with the body and blood of thy Son
**   Jesus Christ our Lord.**
Through him we offer thee our souls
**   and bodies**
to be a living sacrifice.
Send us out
in the power of thy Spirit,
to live and work
to thy praise and glory. Amen.

48 GLORIA IN EXCELSIS may be used, if it has not been used already (the text is printed at section 5); or some other suitable canticle or hymn may be sung.

THE DISMISSAL

49 The priest may say this or an alternative BLESSING (section 54).

The peace of God, which passes all understanding, keep your hearts and minds in the knowledge and love of God, and of his Son Jesus Christ our Lord; and the blessing of God almighty, the Father, the Son, and the Holy Spirit, be among you and remain with you always. **Amen.**

50 Priest   Go in peace and serve the Lord.
    All   **In the name of Christ. Amen.**

or

Priest   Go in the peace of Christ.
All   **Thanks be to God.**

51 The ministers and people depart.

Appendices

PROPER PREFACES FOR THE FIRST THANKSGIVING

Christmas, Presentation, and Annunciation

because thou didst give Jesus Christ thine only Son to be born for our salvation: who, by the operation of the Holy Spirit, was made true man of the substance of the Virgin Mary his mother: and that without spot of sin, to make us clean from all sin.

Epiphany

through Jesus Christ our Lord: who in substance of our mortal flesh manifested forth his glory: that he might bring all men out of darkness into his own marvellous light.

Thursday before Easter

through Jesus Christ our Lord: who having loved his own that were in the world loved them unto the end; and on the night before he suffered, sitting at meat with his disciples, did institute these holy mysteries; that we, redeemed by his death and quickened by his resurrection, might be partakers of his divine nature.

Easter

but chiefly we are bound to praise thee for the glorious resurrection of thy Son Jesus Christ our Lord: for he is the true Paschal Lamb which was offered for us, and has taken away the sin of the world; who by his death has destroyed death, and by his rising to life again has restored to us everlasting life.

Ascension

through thy most dearly beloved Son Jesus Christ our Lord: who after his most glorious resurrection manifestly appeared to all his apostles; and in their sight ascended up into heaven to prepare a place for us; that where he is, thither we might also ascend, and reign with him in glory.

Pentecost

through Jesus Christ our Lord: who after he had ascended up far above all the heavens, and was set down at the right hand of thy majesty, did as at this time send forth upon the universal Church thy holy and life-giving Spirit: that through his glorious power the joy of the everlasting gospel might go forth into all the world; whereby we have been brought out of darkness and error into the clear light and true knowledge of thee, and of thy Son our Saviour Jesus Christ.

Trinity Sunday

who with thine only-begotten Son and the Holy Spirit art one God, one Lord in trinity of Persons and in unity of substance: for that which we believe of thy glory, O Father, the same we believe of thy Son and of the Holy Spirit, without any difference or inequality.

Transfiguration

because the divine glory of the incarnate Word shone forth upon the holy mount before the chosen witnesses of his majesty; and thine own voice from heaven proclaimed thy beloved Son.

Saints' Days

who in the righteousness of thy saints hast given us an example of godly living, and in their blessedness a glorious pledge of the hope of our calling, that, being encompassed about with so great a cloud of witnesses, we may run with patience the race that is set before us, and with them receive the crown of glory that fadeth not away.

Consecration or Dedication of a Church

who, though the heaven of heavens cannot contain thee, and thy glory is in all the world, dost deign to hallow places for thy worship, and in them dost pour forth gifts of grace upon thy faithful people.

Funerals

because through thy Son Jesus Christ our Lord, thou hast given us eternal life, and delivered us from the bondage of sin and the fear of death into the glorious liberty of the children of God.

or

because through thy Son Jesus Christ our Lord, thou hast given us the hope of a glorious resurrection, so that although death comes to us all, yet we rejoice in the promise of eternal life; for to thy faithful people life is changed, not taken away, and when our mortal flesh is laid aside, an everlasting dwelling place is made ready for us in heaven.

53 PROPER PREFACES FOR THE SECOND THANKSGIVING

Advent

And now we give thee thanks, because the day of our deliverance has dawned; and through him thou wilt make all things new, as he comes in power and triumph to judge the world.

Christmas, Presentation, and Annunciation

And now we give thee thanks, for by the operation of the Holy Spirit, he was made man of the Virgin Mary his mother; and that without spot of sin, to make us clean from all sin.

Epiphany

And now we give thee thanks, because in coming to dwell among us as man, he revealed the radiance of his glory, and brought us out of darkness into his own marvellous light.

Lent

And now we give thee thanks, because through him thou hast given us the spirit of discipline, that we may triumph over evil and grow in grace.

Passiontide

And now we give thee thanks, because for our salvation he was obedient even to death on the cross. The tree of defeat became the tree of glory: and where life was lost, there life has been restored.

Thursday before Easter

And now we give thee thanks, because having loved his own that were in the world he loved them unto the end; and on the night before he suffered, sitting at meat with his disciples, did institute these holy mysteries; that we, redeemed by his death and quickened by his resurrection, might be partakers of his divine nature.

Easter

And now we give thee thanks, for his glorious resurrection from the dead. For he is the true Paschal Lamb which was offered for us, and has taken away the sin of the world; who by his death has destroyed death, and by his rising to life again has restored to us everlasting life.

Ascension

And now we give thee thanks, because in his risen body he appeared to his disciples and in their sight was taken into heaven, to reign with thee in glory.

Pentecost

And now we give thee thanks, because by the same Spirit we are led into all truth and are given power to proclaim thy gospel to the nations and to serve thee as a royal priesthood.

Trinity Sunday

And now we give thee thanks, because thou hast revealed thy glory as the glory of thy Son and of the Holy Spirit: three persons equal in majesty, undivided in splendour, yet one Lord, one God, ever to be worshipped and adored.

Transfiguration

And now we give thee thanks, because the divine glory of the incarnate Word shone forth upon the holy mount before the chosen witnesses of his majesty; and thine own voice from heaven proclaimed thy beloved Son.

Saints' Days

And now we give thee thanks, for the glorious pledge of the hope of our calling which thou hast given us in thy saints; that following their example and strengthened by their fellowship, we may run with perseverance the race that is set before us, and with them receive the unfading crown of glory.

Dedication

And now we give thee thanks, for thy blessings on this house of prayer, where we are stirred to faithful witness, and are built up by thy Spirit into a temple made without hands, even the body of thy Son Jesus Christ.

Funerals

And now we give thee thanks, because through him thou hast given us eternal life, and delivered us from the bondage of sin and the fear of death into the glorious liberty of the children of God.

or

And now we give thee thanks, because through him thou hast given us the hope of a glorious resurrection, so that although death comes to us all, yet we rejoice in the promise of eternal life; for to thy faithful people life is changed, not taken away, and when our mortal flesh is laid aside, an everlasting dwelling place is made ready for us in heaven.

54   ALTERNATIVE BLESSINGS

Advent

Christ the Sun of righteousness shine upon you and scatter the darkness from before your path: and the blessing . . .

Christmas

Christ the Son of God gladden your hearts with the good
news of his kingdom: and the blessing . . .

Lent

Christ give you grace to grow in holiness, to deny
yourselves, and to take up your cross, and follow him: and
the blessing . . .

Passiontide

Christ crucified draw you to himself, so that you find in him
a sure ground for faith, a firm support for hope, and the
assurance of sins forgiven: and the blessing . . .

Easter

The God of peace, who brought again from the dead our
Lord Jesus, that great shepherd of the sheep, make you
perfect in every good work to do his will: and the blessing . . .

Ascension

Christ our king make you faithful and strong to do his will,
that you may reign with him in glory: and the blessing . . .

Pentecost

The Spirit of truth lead you into all truth, give you grace to
confess that Jesus Christ is Lord, and to proclaim the word
and works of God: and the blessing . . .

Trinity Sunday

God the Holy Trinity make you strong in faith and love,
defend you on every side, and guide you in truth and peace:
and the blessing . . .

Saints' Days

God give you grace to follow his saints in faith and hope and
love: and the blessing . . .

Unity

Christ the Good Shepherd, who laid down his life for his
sheep, draw you and all who hear his voice to be one within
one fold: and the blessing . . .

55 THE COMMANDMENTS

Minister	God spake these words and said: I am the Lord thy God, thou shalt have none other gods but me.
All	**Lord, have mercy upon us, and incline our hearts to keep this law.**

Minister	Thou shalt not make to thyself any graven image, nor the likeness of anything that is in heaven above, or in the earth beneath, or in the water under the earth. Thou shalt not bow down to them, nor worship them.
All	**Lord, have mercy upon us, and incline our hearts to keep this law.**

Minister	Thou shalt not take the name of the Lord thy God in vain.
All	**Lord, have mercy upon us, and incline our hearts to keep this law.**

Minister	Remember that thou keep holy the Sabbath day. Six days shalt thou labour, and do all that thou hast to do; but the seventh day is the Sabbath of the Lord thy God.
All	**Lord, have mercy upon us, and incline our hearts to keep this law.**

Minister	Honour thy father and thy mother.
All	**Lord, have mercy upon us, and incline our hearts to keep this law.**

Minister	Thou shalt do no murder.
All	**Lord, have mercy upon us, and incline our hearts to keep this law.**

Minister	Thou shalt not commit adultery.
All	**Lord, have mercy upon us, and incline our hearts to keep this law.**

Minister	Thou shalt not steal.
All	**Lord, have mercy upon us,**
	and incline our hearts to keep this law.

Minister	Thou shalt not bear false witness.
All	**Lord, have mercy upon us,**
	and incline our hearts to keep this law.

Minister	Thou shalt not covet.
All	**Lord, have mercy upon us,**
	and write all these thy laws in our hearts,
	we beseech thee.

56 THE SUMMARY OF THE LAW

Minister	Our Lord Jesus Christ said: Hear, O Israel, the Lord our God is one Lord; and thou shalt love the Lord thy God with all thy heart, and with all thy soul, and with all thy mind, and with all thy strength. This is the first commandment. And the second is like, namely this: Thou shalt love thy neighbour as thyself. There is none other commandment greater than these. On these two commandments hang all the law and the prophets.
All	**Lord, have mercy upon us,**
	and write all these thy laws in our hearts,
	we beseech thee.

57 KYRIE ELEISON

Lord, have mercy (upon us.)	Kyrie eleison.
Lord, have mercy (upon us.)	**Kyrie eleison.**
Lord, have mercy (upon us.)	Kyrie eleison.

Christ, have mercy (upon us.)	**Christe eleison.**
Christ, have mercy (upon us.)	Christe eleison.
Christ, have mercy (upon us.)	**Christe eleison.**

Lord, have mercy (upon us.)	Kyrie eleison.
Lord, have mercy (upon us.)	**Kyrie eleison.**
Lord, have mercy (upon us.)	Kyrie eleison.

Either of the following prayers may be used instead of those in sections 46 and 47.

Priest

O Lord and heavenly Father, we thy humble servants entirely desire thy fatherly goodness mercifully to accept this our sacrifice of praise and thanksgiving; most humbly beseeching thee to grant that by the merits and death of thy Son Jesus Christ, and through faith in his blood, we and all thy whole Church may obtain remission of our sins, and all other benefits of his passion. And here we offer and present unto thee, O Lord, ourselves, our souls and bodies, to be a reasonable, holy, and lively sacrifice unto thee; humbly beseeching thee, that all we, who are partakers of this Holy Communion, may be fulfilled with thy grace and heavenly benediction. And although we be unworthy, through our manifold sins, to offer unto thee any sacrifice, yet we beseech thee to accept this our bounden duty and service, not weighing our merits, but pardoning our offences; through Jesus Christ our Lord, by whom, and with whom, in the unity of the Holy Ghost, all honour and glory be unto thee, O Father almighty, world without end. **Amen.**

All

**Almighty Lord, and everlasting God,
we offer and present unto thee ourselves,
    our souls and bodies,
to be a reasonable, holy, and living
    sacrifice unto thee:
humbly beseeching thee,
that all we, who are partakers of this Holy
    Communion,
may be fulfilled with thy grace and heavenly
    benediction.
And although we be unworthy, through our
    manifold sins,**

to offer unto thee any sacrifice,
yet we beseech thee to accept this our bounden
   duty and service,
not weighing our merits, but pardoning our
   offences;
through Jesus Christ our Lord,
to whom, with thee and the Holy Ghost,
be all honour and glory, world without end.
Amen.

Initiation Services

Thanksgiving for the Birth of a Child
Thanksgiving after Adoption

NOTES

1 **Explanation** Unless Baptism is to follow immediately, the minister shall explain to the parents or adoptive parents on some occasion before the service or after sections 4 or 20, that the service of thanksgiving is not baptism, which is the sacrament instituted by Christ for those who wish to become members of his Church.

2 **The Place** These services should normally be used in church. Use in the home or in hospital is permitted at the discretion of the priest.

3 **The Presence of the Family** Whenever possible, in addition to both parents or adoptive parents and the child, any other children of the family should be present.

4 **Holy Communion, or Morning and Evening Prayer** These services may be used at Holy Communion or at Morning or Evening Prayer.
At Holy Communion they may be used either at the beginning of the service or after the Sermon; and the Prayers of Intercession may be omitted.
At Morning or Evening Prayer they may be used either at the beginning of the service or after the Second Reading or after the Sermon.

5 **Additional Material** If these services are used on their own, the minister may add suitable hymns and scripture readings (see sections 16 and 29) and a sermon.

6 **Baptism** If these services are to be followed immediately by Baptism, it is sufficient to use, after a birth, sections 1-3; after an adoption, sections 17-19, 23–25.

Thanksgiving for the Birth of a Child

1   Minister   Let us thank God that in his goodness
he has given you *this son/daughter*.

                      God our Father,
maker of all that is living,
we praise you for the wonder and joy
     of creation.
We thank you from our hearts
for the life of *this child*,
for a safe delivery,
and for the privilege of parenthood.
Accept our thanks and praise
through Jesus Christ our Lord. **Amen.**

2   The parents of the *child* may say together

                      God our Father,
in giving us *this child*
you have shown us your love.
Help us to be trustworthy parents.
Make us patient and understanding,
that our *child* may always be sure of
     our love
and grow up to be happy and responsible;
through Jesus Christ our Lord. **Amen.**

3   The following VERSICLES AND RESPONSES are said,
or PSALM 100.

     Minister   My soul proclaims the greatness of the Lord,
     All   **my spirit rejoices in God my saviour.**

     Minister   Glory and honour and power
are yours by right, O Lord our God;
     All   **for you created all things,
and by your will they have their being.**

Minister	Holy, holy, holy is God the sovereign Lord of all,
All	**who is, and who was, and who is to come.**

Minister	Great and marvellous are your deeds, O Lord God,
All	**just and true are your ways, O King of the ages.**

Minister	Praise our God, all you his servants,
All	**you that fear him, both great and small.**

Minister	His mercy rests on those who fear him,
All	**now and for countless ages. Amen.**

PSALM 100

1 **O shout to the Lord in triumph ᛁ all the ᛁ earth:**
 serve the Lord with gladness
 and come before his ᛁ face with ᛁ songs of ᛁ joy.

2 **Know that the Lord ᛁ he is ᛁ God:**
 it is he who has made us and we are his
 we are his ᛁ people · and the ᛁ sheep of · his ᛁ pasture.

3 **Come into his gates with thanksgiving**
 and into his ᛁ courts with ᛁ praise:
 give thanks to him and ᛁ bless his ᛁ holy ᛁ name.

4 **For the Lord is good * his loving mercy ᛁ is for ᛁ ever:**
 his faithfulness through ᛁ out all ᛁ gener ᛁ ations.

Glory to the Father and ᛁ to the ᛁ Son:
 and ᛁ to the ᛁ Holy ᛁ Spirit;
as it was in the be ᛁ ginning is ᛁ now:
 and shall be for ᛁ ever. ᛁ A ᛁ men.

or A HYMN may be sung.

4   Minister

Hear these words from the Gospel according to St Mark:
They brought children for Jesus to touch. The disciples
rebuked them, but when Jesus saw this he was indignant
and said to them, 'Let the children come to me; do not try to
stop them; for the kingdom of God belongs to such as these.
I tell you, whoever does not accept the kingdom of God like a
child will never enter it.' And he put his arms round them,
laid his hands upon them, and blessed them.
Mark 10.13-16 NEB

5   The minister may give a copy of one of the gospels to the
parents, saying

This book contains the Good News of God's
love. Read it, for it tells how you and your family
can share in eternal life, through repentance and
faith in Jesus Christ.

6   Minister   Jesus taught us to call God our Father,
and so in faith and trust we say

All Our Father in heaven,   or   Our Father, who art in heaven,
hallowed be your name,   hallowed be thy name;
your kingdom come,   thy kingdom come;
your will be done,   thy will be done;
on earth as in heaven.   on earth as it is in heaven.
Give us today our daily bread.   Give us this day our daily bread.
Forgive us our sins   And forgive us our trespasses,
as we forgive those   as we forgive those
  who sin against us.   who trespass against us.
Lead us not into temptation   And lead us not into temptation;
but deliver us from evil.   but deliver us from evil.

For the kingdom, the power,   For thine is the kingdom,
  and the glory are yours   the power, and the glory,
now and for ever. Amen.   for ever and ever. Amen.

7   Minister   Almighty God, look with favour on *this child*;
grant that, being nourished with all goodness,
he may grow in discipline and grace until *he*
comes to the fullness of faith; through Jesus
Christ our Lord. **Amen.**

Thanksgiving for the Birth of a Child · 215

8 The minister then says one or more of these prayers.

9 Heavenly Father, whose blessed Son shared at Nazareth the life of an earthly home: bless the *home* of *this child,* and help all *the family* to live together in your love. Teach them to serve you and each other, and make them always ready to show your love to those in need; for the sake of Jesus Christ our Lord. **Amen.**

10 Father in heaven, bless these parents, that they may cherish their *child*; make them wise and understanding, to help *him* as *he grows,* and surround *this family* with the light of your truth and the warmth of your love; through Jesus Christ our Lord. **Amen.**

11 Almighty Father, we thank you that you have made the love of Christ for his bride the Church to be a pattern for the marriage of husband and wife. We pray that these your servants may grow in love and self-giving to each other all the days of their life; through Jesus Christ our Lord. **Amen.**

12 God our Father, we pray to you for all who have the care of *this child.* Guide them with your Holy Spirit, that they may bring *him* up in the ways of truth and love. Through their care enable *him* to grow in grace and become daily more like your Son, our Saviour Jesus Christ. **Amen.**

13 Almighty God, the fountain of all wisdom, you know our needs before we ask, and our ignorance in asking. Have compassion on our weakness, and give us those things which for our unworthiness we dare not and for our blindness we cannot ask, for the sake of your Son, Jesus Christ our Lord. **Amen.**

14   This prayer may be said by all.

> **God our Father,**
> **we pray for** *this child*,
> **that in due time**
> *he* **may be received by baptism**
> **into the family of your Church,**
> **and become** *an inheritor* **of your kingdom;**
> **through Jesus Christ our Lord. Amen.**

15   The minister ends the service with one of these BLESSINGS.

> The Lord bless you and watch over you,
> the Lord make his face shine upon you
> and be gracious to you,
> the Lord look kindly on you and give you peace;
> and the blessing of God almighty,
> the Father, the Son, and the Holy Spirit,
> be among you and remain with you always.
> **Amen.**

or

> The love of the Lord Jesus
> draw you to himself,
> the power of the Lord Jesus
> strengthen you in his service,
> the joy of the Lord Jesus fill your hearts;
> and the blessing of God almighty,
> the Father, the Son, and the Holy Spirit,
> be among you and remain with you always.
> **Amen.**

16   When this service is used on its own (see note 5), readings may be chosen from the following.

Genesis 1.26-28, 31a	1 Samuel 1.20-end
Tobit 8.5-6	
Romans 8.28-30	Romans 12.1, 2
Ephesians 3.14-21	
Matthew 7.24-27	Luke 2.22, 28a (28b-35)
John 15.9-12	

Thanksgiving after Adoption

17   Minister   Let us thank God that in his goodness
he has given you *this son/daughter*.

God our Father,
maker of all that is living,
we praise you for the wonder and joy
   of creation.
We thank you from our hearts
for the life of *this child*,
and for the privilege of parenthood.
Accept our thanks and praise
through Jesus Christ our Lord. **Amen.**

18   The parents of the *child* may say together

God our Father,
in giving us *this child*
you have shown us your love.
Help us to be trustworthy parents.
Make us patient and understanding,
that our *child* may always be sure of
   our love,
and grow up to be happy and responsible;
through Jesus Christ our Lord. **Amen.**

19   The following VERSICLES AND RESPONSES are said,
or PSALM 100.

Minister   My soul proclaims the greatness of the Lord,
All   **my spirit rejoices in God my saviour.**

Minister   Glory and honour and power
are yours by right, O Lord our God;
All   **for you created all things,
and by your will they have their being.**

Minister	Holy, holy, holy is God the sovereign Lord of all,
All	**who is, and who was, and who is to come.**

Minister	Great and marvellous are your deeds, O Lord God,
All	**just and true are your ways, O King of the ages.**

Minister	Praise our God, all you his servants,
All	**you that fear him, both great and small.**

Minister	His mercy rests on those who fear him,
All	**now and for countless ages. Amen.**

PSALM 100

1 **O shout to the Lord in triumph ᴵ all the ᴵ earth:**
   serve the Lord with gladness
   and come before his ᴵ face with ᴵ songs of ᴵ joy.

2 **Know that the Lord ᴵ he is ᴵ God:**
   it is he who has made us and we are his
   we are his ᴵ people · and the ᴵ sheep of · his ᴵ pasture.

3 **Come into his gates with thanksgiving**
   and into his ᴵ courts with ᴵ praise:
   give thanks to him and ᴵ bless his ᴵ holy ᴵ name.

4 **For the Lord is good * his loving mercy ᴵ is for ᴵ ever:**
   his faithfulness through ᴵout all ᴵ gener ᴵations.

Glory to the Father and ᴵ to the ᴵ Son:
   and ᴵ to the ᴵ Holy ᴵ Spirit;
as it was in the be ᴵginning is ᴵ now:
   and shall be for ᶦ ever. ᵀ A ᴵ men.

or A HYMN may be sung.

20   Minister

Hear these words from the Gospel according to St Mark:
They brought children for Jesus to touch. The disciples
rebuked them, but when Jesus saw this he was indignant
and said to them, 'Let the children come to me; do not try to
stop them; for the kingdom of God belongs to such as these.
I tell you, whoever does not accept the kingdom of God like a
child will never enter it.' And he put his arms round them,
laid his hands upon them, and blessed them.
Mark 10.13-16 NEB

21   The minister may give a copy of one of the gospels to the
      parents, saying

                    This book contains the Good News of God's
                    love. Read it, for it tells how you and your family
                    can share in eternal life, through repentance and
                    faith in Jesus Christ.

22   Minister   Jesus taught us to call God our Father,
                   and so in faith and trust we say

All   **Our Father in heaven,**   **or** **Our Father, who art in heaven,**
      hallowed be your name,   **hallowed be thy name;**
      your kingdom come,   **thy kingdom come;**
      your will be done,   **thy will be done;**
      on earth as in heaven.   **on earth as it is in heaven.**
      Give us today our daily bread.   **Give us this day our daily bread.**
      Forgive us our sins   **And forgive us our trespasses,**
      as we forgive those   **as we forgive those**
        who sin against us.   **who trespass against us.**
      Lead us not into temptation   **And lead us not into temptation;**
      but deliver us from evil.   **but deliver us from evil.**

      For the kingdom, the power,   **For thine is the kingdom,**
        and the glory are yours   **the power, and the glory,**
      now and for ever. Amen.   **for ever and ever. Amen.**

23   Minister   Almighty God, look with favour on *this child*;
                   grant that, being nourished with all goodness,
                   he may grow in discipline and grace until *he*
                   comes to the fullness of faith; through Jesus
                   Christ our Lord. **Amen.**

      220   Thanksgiving after Adoption

24   God, whose nature is always to have mercy,
            look down with love on the natural father and
            mother of *this child*; keep them in your good
            providence, and give them your peace in their
            hearts; through Jesus Christ our Lord. **Amen.**

25   The members of the family then say together

            We receive *this child* into our family with
            thanksgiving and joy.
            Through the love of God we receive *him*;
            with the love of God we will care for *him*;
            by the love of God we will guide *him*;
            and in the love of God may we all abide for
            ever. **Amen.**

26   Minister   Heavenly Father, whose blessed Son shared at
            Nazareth the life of an earthly home: bless the
            home of *this child,* and help all *the family* to live
            together in your love. Teach them to serve you
            and each other, and make them always ready to
            show your love to those in need; for the sake of
            Jesus Christ our Lord. **Amen.**

27   This prayer may be said by all.

            God our Father,
            we pray for *this child* **,**
            that in due time
            he **may be received by baptism**
            into the family of your Church,
            and become *an inheritor* **of your kingdom;**
            through Jesus Christ our Lord. Amen.

28   The minister ends the service with one of these BLESSINGS.

            The Lord bless you and watch over you,
            the Lord make his face shine upon you
            and be gracious to you,
            the Lord look kindly on you and give you peace;

and the blessing of God almighty,
the Father, the Son, and the Holy Spirit,
be among you and remain with you always.
Amen.

or

The love of the Lord Jesus
draw you to himself,
the power of the Lord Jesus
strengthen you in his service,
the joy of the Lord Jesus fill your hearts;
and the blessing of God almighty,
the Father, the Son, and the Holy Spirit,
be among you and remain with you always.
Amen.

29   When this service is used on its own (see note 5), readings
may be chosen from the following.

Genesis 1.26-28, 31a	1 Samuel 1.20-end
Tobit 8.5-6	
Romans 8.28-30	Romans 12.1, 2
Ephesians 3.14-21	
Matthew 7.24-27	Luke 2.22, 28a (28b-35)
John 15.9-12	

The Baptism of Children

NOTES

1   **The Administration of Baptism** Holy Baptism is normally administered by the parish priest in the course of public worship on Sunday; but it may be administered at other times, and he may delegate its administration to other lawful ministers. Where rubrics indicate that a passage is to be said by 'the priest', this must be understood to include any other minister authorized to administer Holy Baptism.

2   **The Answering of the Questions** When children who are old enough to respond are baptized, the parents and godparents answer the questions (sections 48 and 53), and at the discretion of the priest the children may also answer them.

3   **The Signing with the Cross** The signing with the cross may take place either at section 49 or at section 56. The sign of the cross may be made in oil blessed for this purpose.

4   **The Giving of a Candle** A lighted candle, which may be the paschal candle, may be made ready so that other candles may be lighted from it.

5   **The Use of the Candidate's Name** At the signing with the cross and the giving of a candle, the priest or other minister may address the candidate by name.

6   **The People's Responses** At the signing with the cross it is sufficient if the people join in and say their part (sections 49 and 56) once only, when all have been signed; and if a candle is given to those who have been baptized, it is sufficient if the people join in and say their part (section 57) once only, when all have received a candle.

7   **The Attendance of the People** This order of service should normally be used at Holy Communion or Morning or Evening Prayer. At other times representatives of the

regular congregation should attend the service, so that they may welcome the newly baptized (section 58) and be put in mind of their own baptism.

8   **Hymns** If occasion requires, hymns may be sung at points other than those which are indicated in this order.

9   **The Administration of the Water** A threefold administration of water (whether by dipping or pouring) is a very ancient practice of the Church, and is commended as testifying to the faith of the Trinity in which candidates are baptized. Nevertheless, a single administration is also lawful and valid.

10 **Alternative Readings** Section 45 may be omitted and either Matthew 28.16-20 or John 3.1-8 read in its place.

The Baptism of Children

42 The priest says

> Children who are too young to profess the Christian faith are baptized on the understanding that they are brought up as Christians within the family of the Church.
>
> As they grow up, they need the help and encouragement of that family, so that they learn to be faithful in public worship and private prayer, to live by trust in God, and come to confirmation.
>
> Parents and godparents, the *children* whom you have brought for baptism *depend* chiefly on you for the help and encouragement *they need*. Are you willing to give it to *them* by your prayers, by your example, and by your teaching?

Parents and godparents

> **I am willing.**

43 And if the *child is* old enough to understand, the priest speaks to *him* in these or similar words.

> *N*, when you are baptized, you become *a member* of a new family. God takes you for his own *child*, and all Christian people will be your brothers and sisters.

THE MINISTRY OF THE WORD

Sections 44, 45, and 46 may be omitted when Baptism is administered at Holy Communion or at Morning or Evening Prayer.

44   Priest   The Lord is loving to everyone;
         All   **and his mercy is over all his works.**

45   Priest

God is the creator of all things, and by the birth of children he gives to parents a share in the work and joy of creation. But we who are born of earthly parents need to be born again. For in the Gospel Jesus tells us that unless a man has been born again, he cannot see the Kingdom of God. And so God gives us the way to a second birth, a new creation and life in union with him.

Baptism is the sign and seal of this new birth. In St Matthew's Gospel we read of the risen Christ commanding his followers to make disciples of all nations and to baptize men everywhere; and in the Acts of the Apostles we read of St Peter preaching in these words: 'Repent and be baptized in the name of Jesus Christ for the forgiveness of sins; and you shall receive the gift of the Holy Spirit. For the promise is to you and your children and to all that are afar off, everyone whom the Lord calls to him.'

In obedience to this same command we ourselves were baptized and now bring *these children* to baptism.

46   Priest   We thank God therefore for our baptism to life in Christ, and we pray for *these children (N)* and say together
         All   **Heavenly Father, in your love**
                       you have called us to know you,
                       led us to trust you,
                       and bound our life with yours.
                       Surround *these children* with your love;
                       protect *them* from evil;
                       fill *them* with your Holy Spirit;

and receive *them* **into the family of your Church;**
that *they* **may walk with us in the way of Christ**
and grow in the knowledge of your love. Amen.

THE DECISION

47 The parents and godparents stand, and the priest says
to them

Those who bring children to be baptized must
affirm their allegiance to Christ and their
rejection of all that is evil.

It is your duty to bring up *these children* to fight
against evil and to follow Christ.

48 Therefore I ask these questions which you must
answer for yourselves and for *these children*.

Do you turn to Christ?
Answer **I turn to Christ.**

Do you repent of your sins?
Answer **I repent of my sins.**

Do you renounce evil?
Answer **I renounce evil.**

49 Either here or at section 56 the priest makes THE SIGN OF
THE CROSS on the forehead of each child, saying to each

I sign you with the cross, the sign of Christ.

After the signing of each or all, he says

Do not be ashamed to confess the faith of Christ
crucified.
All **Fight valiantly under the banner of Christ**
against sin, the world, and the devil,
and continue his faithful *soldiers* **and** *servants*
to the end of your *lives.*

| 50 | Priest | May almighty God deliver you from the powers of darkness, and lead you in the light and obedience of Christ. **Amen.** |

51 A HYMN or PSALM may be sung.

THE BAPTISM

52 The priest stands before the water of baptism and says

| | | Praise God who made heaven and earth, |
| | **All** | **who keeps his promise for ever.** |

| | Priest | Almighty God, whose Son Jesus Christ was baptized in the river Jordan:
we thank you for the gift of water to cleanse us and revive us;
we thank you that through the waters of the Red Sea, you led your people out of slavery to freedom in the promised land;
we thank you that through the deep waters of death you brought your Son, and raised him to life in triumph.
Bless this water, that your *servants* who *are* washed in it may be made one with Christ in his death and in his resurrection, to be cleansed and delivered from all sin.
Send your Holy Spirit upon *them* to bring *them* to new birth in the family of your Church, and raise *them* with Christ to full and eternal life.
For all might, majesty, authority, and power are yours, now and for ever. **Amen.** |

53 The priest says to the parents and godparents

You have brought *these children* to baptism. You must now declare before God and his Church the Christian faith into which *they are* to be baptized, and in which you will help *them* to grow. You must answer for yourselves and for *these children*.

Do you believe and trust in God the Father, who made the world?

Answer **I believe and trust in him.**

Do you believe and trust in his Son Jesus Christ, who redeemed mankind?

Answer **I believe and trust in him.**

Do you believe and trust in his Holy Spirit, who gives life to the people of God?

Answer **I believe and trust in him.**

54 The priest turns to the congregation and says

This is the faith of the Church.

All **This is our faith.**
We believe and trust in one God,
Father, Son, and Holy Spirit.

55 The parents and godparents being present with each child, the priest baptizes *him*. He dips *him* in the water or pours water on *him*, addressing *him* by name.

N, I baptize you in the name of the Father, and of the Son, and of the Holy Spirit.

And each one of *his* sponsors answers

Amen.

56 The priest makes THE SIGN OF THE CROSS on the forehead of each child if he has not already done so. The appropriate words are printed at section 49.

57 The priest or other person may give to a parent or godparent for each child A LIGHTED CANDLE, saying to each

Receive this light.

And when a candle has been given to each one, he says

This is to show that you have passed
from darkness to light.
All **Shine as a light in the world**
to the glory of God the Father.

THE WELCOME

58 The priest and the congregation, representing the whole Church, welcome the newly baptized.

Priest God has received you by baptism into
his Church.
All **We welcome you into the Lord's Family.**
We are members together of the body of Christ;
we are children of the same heavenly Father;
we are inheritors together of the kingdom
of God.
We welcome you.

THE PRAYERS

59 The prayers that follow are omitted when Baptism is administered at Holy Communion; and may be omitted when Baptism is administered at Morning or Evening Prayer.

Priest Lord God our Father, maker of heaven and
earth, we thank you that by your Holy Spirit
these children have been born again into new life,
adopted for your own, and received into the
fellowship of your Church:
grant that *they* may grow in the faith
into which *they have* been baptized,
that *they* may profess it for *themselves*

when *they come* to be confirmed,
and that all things belonging to the Spirit
may live and grow in *them*. **Amen.**

60 Priest   Heavenly Father, we pray for the parents of *these
children*; give them the spirit of wisdom and
love, that their *homes* may reflect the joy of your
eternal kingdom. **Amen.**

61 Priest   Almighty God, we thank you for our fellowship
in the household of faith with all those who have
been baptized in your name. Keep us faithful to
our baptism, and so make us ready for that day
when the whole creation shall be made perfect
in your Son, our Saviour Jesus Christ. **Amen.**

62 Priest   Jesus taught us to call God our Father,
and so in faith and trust we say

All **Our Father in heaven,**   or   **Our Father, who art in heaven,**
hallowed be your name,   **hallowed be thy name;**
your kingdom come,   **thy kingdom come;**
your will be done,   **thy will be done;**
on earth as in heaven.   **on earth as it is in heaven.**
Give us today our daily bread.   **Give us this day our daily bread.**
Forgive us our sins   **And forgive us our trespasses,**
as we forgive those   **as we forgive those**
who sin against us.   **who trespass against us.**
Lead us not into temptation   **And lead us not into temptation;**
but deliver us from evil.   **but deliver us from evil.**

For the kingdom, the power,   **For thine is the kingdom,**
and the glory are yours   **the power, and the glory,**
now and for ever. Amen.   **for ever and ever. Amen.**

63 Priest   The grace of our Lord Jesus Christ, and the love
of God, and the fellowship of the Holy Spirit be
with us all evermore. **Amen.**

COPYRIGHT

The Alternative Service Book 1980 (the ASB) and the individual services in it are copyright © The Central Board of Finance of the Church of England 1980.

Psalms printed within the services reproduced from the ASB follow the text and pointing of The Liturgical Psalter, which is published separately as *The Psalms: a new translation for worship*, © English text 1976, 1977, David L Frost, John A Emerton, Andrew A Macintosh, all rights reserved, © pointing 1976, 1977 William Collins Sons & Co Ltd.

The texts of the Nicene Creed (adapted) and the Gloria in Excelsis, the Sanctus and Benedictus, and the Agnus Dei, as they appear in the Order for Holy Communion Rite A, and the texts of the Apostles' Creed and the Canticles Benedictus, Te Deum (adapted), Magnificat and Nunc Dimittis, as printed in Morning Prayer and Evening Prayer, are copyright © 1970, 1971, 1975 International Consultation on English Texts (ICET). The Lord's Prayer in its modern form is adapted from the ICET version.

The material from the ASB reproduced in this book also includes the following material (some in adapted form):

Material from The Book of Common Prayer, the text of which is the property of the Crown in perpetuity;

The Song of Christ's Glory, from the South African Daily Office, the copyright in which is held by the Church of the Province of Southern Africa;

A Collect from *The Daily Office Revised* by the Joint Liturgical Group (of Churches in Great Britain);

'O gladsome light, O grace', translated by Robert Bridges (1844–1930), from the *Yattendon Hymnal*.

Reproduction of material from *The Alternative Service Book 1980*.

New arrangements apply to local editions from 1 January 1988. They cover both reproduction for a single occasion and reproduction for repeated use. Details of the arrangements for reproducing services from *The Alternative Service Book 1980* on a non-commercial basis are available in a leaflet *Liturgical Texts for Local Use: Guidelines and Copyright Information.* This can be obtained by post (please send stamped addressed envelope) from The Copyright Administrator, Central Board of Finance, Church House, Great Smith Street, London SW1P 3NZ.

All other copyright inquiries relating to *The Alternative Service Book 1980* should be addressed to The Copyright Administrator at Church House (see above).